#ME TOO

IN THE CORPORATE WORLD

Also by Sylvia Ann Hewlett

The Sponsor Effect: How to be a Better Leader by Investing in Others

Forget a Mentor, Find a Sponsor: The New Way to Fast-Track Your Career

Executive Presence: The Missing Link Between Merit and Success

Off-Ramps and On-Ramps: Keeping Talented Women on the Road to Success

Creating a Life: What Every Women Needs to Know about Having a Baby and a Career

The War Against Parents (coauthored with Cornel West)

When the Bough Breaks: The Cost of Neglecting Our Children

#ME
TOO

IN THE
CORPORATE
WORLD

Power, Privilege, and the Path Forward

Sylvia Ann Hewlett

HARPER
BUSINESS

An Imprint of HarperCollins*Publishers*

HarperCollins books may be purchased for educational, business, or sales promotional use. For information, please email the Special Markets Department at SPsales@harpercollins.com.

FIRST EDITION

Designed by Bonni Leon-Berman

Library of Congress Cataloging-in-Publication Data has been applied for.

ISBN 978-0-06-289919-4

20 21 22 23 24   LSC   10 9 8 7 6 5 4 3 2 1

For my daughters and granddaughters: Shira, Lisa, Emma, Anais, Anika, and Amalia. May they be fierce and fearless in pursuit of their dreams.

CONTENTS

PREFACE

It was Friday afternoon in late January and I was chomping at the bit, eager to leave the office. I had turned twenty-three two days earlier and had a celebration to get to. My sister was throwing a party for me at the flat we shared in West Hampstead. I wanted to get home to help her set up.

I checked my watch—for the umpteenth time. It was only 4:30 p.m., still too early to walk out the door. As a new employee (just three months on the job) I felt obligated to stick around until at least 5:30. I opened up a data file I was working on and attempted to settle down.

A few minutes later there was a tap on the frosted glass panel that ran along the side of my desk. Sebastian Tyler's[*] large head loomed over the edge of my cubicle. "Come join me for a drink," he boomed, thrusting his face uncomfortably close to mine. I shrank back, trying to avoid spittle as well as a lewd leer. "Five o'clock sharp, something strong." Sebastian wet his fleshy lips and stared at me. "I think you know where my office is."

Beating back shock and surprise, I made my excuses: "Afraid that can't work, Mr. Tyler. I need to leave a little early today. It was my birthday earlier this week and I have plans with friends." Sebastian straightened up and pondered. Then, with a salacious grin and an air of triumph, he thrust his face into mine again. "Tell you what. I'll be very happy with a hand job, and that won't

[*] Name has been changed.

take very long. Come along about 4:45 p.m. and you'll be out of here in a jiffy." Sebastian let out a snort of satisfaction, turned on his heel, and left—leaving me reeling.

I fled to the ladies' room and rinsed my hands and face—three times. I took the stairs, left the building by the side door, and headed to the Underground. Before getting on the tube at Green Park, I stopped for a cup of tea at Lyons to steady my nerves before heading home.

I was gobsmacked. There had been no lead-up to Sebastian's crude proposition. He was the boss of my boss, and I hardly knew him. We'd had one previous encounter. In mid-December, at the firm's Christmas party, I'd somehow ended up in a stilted conversation with him and his wife, Ava. What did this over-weight, sweaty, married man, twice my age think he was doing? Did he really imagine that I fancied him? Sebastian's arrogance and entitlement were breathtaking.

I was also ashamed. Had I somehow signaled I was available for "hand jobs" on Friday afternoons? I was pretty sure I didn't come across as a siren. My go-to office outfits were Ann Taylor suits and high-necked blouses. I didn't wear "come hither" shoes or crack jokes with sexual innuendos. Yet even though I couldn't put my finger on the reason why, I still felt complicit, deserving of shame and blame.

But most of all, I was scared. How the heck was I going to fight off Sebastian?

He had enormous power over me. Sebastian was on the man-agement committee of the prominent consultancy where I worked and could make or break my fledgling career. I could only imagine how vindictive he'd be if I had the temerity to reject his advances. He was so full of himself he probably thought he was doing me a favor by inviting me to give him a "hand job" at the end of the working day! This huge sense of entitlement would spur him to retaliate viciously. He'd probably throw me out on my ear without a reference and therefore no prospect of landing another job in the consulting sector.

By the time I left the tea shop that Friday afternoon, I had made two decisions. I would deal with my shame and self-blame by keeping quiet—not telling anyone. I reckoned that would reduce the humiliation and the cost to friends and family. I would also do my level best to dodge Sebastian—keep out of his way and hope he would go away. If he persisted, I would turn him down. I couldn't live with myself if I caved in to his demands.

Over the next couple of weeks a few things unfolded.

Sebastian did not let up. The following Wednesday I attended a division-wide, end-of-month planning session led by Sebastian and the CEO of the firm. The meeting ended at noon. As participants collected their notes and headed for the door, Sebastian peered over his bifocals, waved in my direction, and said loudly, "See that new girl? Now she has a *smashing* figure. There's definitely an upside to hiring women." He chortled, and several other male executives joined in. Deeply embarrassed, I pretended I hadn't heard and slipped out of the room.

Two days later, Sebastian sidled up behind me as I was standing in the lunch line in the cafeteria. With a dozen or so colleagues looking on, he whispered in my ear, slapped my bottom two or three times, and walked away laughing. I was beyond mortified. The slaps were bad enough, but even more humiliating were the ways he affected familiarity and ownership. It was as though he wanted everyone to think that we had a sexual thing going on, that I belonged to him.

He made that point even more brutally later that day. It was midafternoon and I was in what was called the "Xeroxing room," copying some documents, when Sebastian walked in. After checking that no one else was around, he closed the door, turned off the lights, and grabbed me. He went for my breasts, yanking on them, pulling them out of my blouse and my bra. He then began squeezing and twisting my nipples. I let out a loud squeal of pain—which seemed to bring him to his senses. A slobbering kiss and he was gone, leaving me a wreck.

Trembling, I stayed quiet for a few minutes and focused on just breathing. I then smoothed my hair and went to work to deal with the blouse situation—it was missing three buttons, so I used paper clips to hold it together. But my ordeal wasn't over. When I emerged from that small dark room, I encountered a queue of curious coworkers. Sebastian had spread the word that I had been hit with a debilitating migraine, had retreated to the Xeroxing room, and was not to be disturbed. Of course, no one believed him. As I scuttled by this line of male colleagues, they took in my flushed face and tattered blouse and made judgments.

People gossiped. Rumors spread. Before long nearly all of my immediate colleagues believed that I was having an affair with Sebastian. They became wary of me, afraid to share work-related problems for fear that I would tell on them to the big boss. They also became resentful, convinced that I now had unfair advantages and would be first in line for a pay hike or promotion. Shunned and surrounded by suspicion, I became totally isolated. No one was willing to look at my draft reports, involve me in new projects, invite me to client meetings, or even grab a coffee with me.

I was at my wits' end. I figured it was useless to go to HR, widely seen as feeble and in the pocket of senior management. The top brass would simply protect one of their own. So I approached the professor who had recommended me for my consulting job—someone who had supervised my honors thesis and knew quite a bit about my ambitions and capabilities. We made an appointment, and I traveled up to Cambridge to get his help.

Over tea and biscuits I told him of the poisonous brew I was facing at work, how harassment and isolation were making it difficult to do my job. I asked him: Did he know any other senior executives at the firm, and if so, could he appeal to them on my behalf? I needed one or two of the top dogs to rein Sebastian in. Professor Coe*—a kindly man—gave me his full attention. At the end of my appeal, he pushed his teacup aside, sighed deeply, and told me the bad news.

"Best get out of there. Sebastian is a prick—I've known him for twenty years, and he's always been a prick. But the fact is, he's the biggest producer and runs the show. I do know one or two chaps at the top, but they wouldn't intervene."

The next day I handed in my notice. By the middle of March I was gone.

I remember well the day I packed up my desk and walked out of the firm's offices in St. James's. I felt the defeat bitterly. I had grown up in a working-class family, and it had been a long, hard journey from my coal-mining village in South Wales to Cambridge University and a job at a blue-chip consulting firm. Aside from the prestige and salary, I loved what I did at work every day. Whether the challenge was how to drive low-tech solutions in Africa or how to create greater access to microfinance in Asia, I delighted in finding concrete solutions to real-world problems.

But don't get me wrong—back then and also today I don't see myself as one of the more serious casualties of sexual abuse. My career was sideswiped but not snuffed out by Sebastian Tyler. After my forced exit from consulting, I returned to academia. Three years later, PhD in hand, I embarked on a college teaching

---

* Name has been changed.

career. It was a fine way forward, even if not nearly as good a fit for me as the first career I had chosen. I missed the immediacy and the impact of my old job.

My #MeToo moment lay dormant for decades. It was awoken on October 28, 2017. The occasion was a leadership conference in New York City, where I joined Arianna Huffington for a "fireside chat" on sexual harassment in Silicon Valley. I remember the buzz as we walked onto the stage, the two hundred–odd executives in the room on the edge of their chairs, eager to hear what Arianna had to say. The scandal at Uber was unfolding, and Arianna, who was on the Uber board, had been center stage in a recent move to oust CEO Travis Kalanick. He had been accused of turning a blind eye to sexual harassment and creating a toxic environment for women.

In her famously husky voice, Arianna spoke eloquently about the need to bring down "brilliant jerks" who behave badly. In her view, Silicon Valley worshipped a breed of young male entrepreneurs with hard-core engineering skills who made billions for themselves and their companies. They had become untouchable and could get away with anything. But unless these megastars were called to account for sexual abuse, women would continue to languish and leave the tech sector.

Memories snapped into place in my mind and Sebastian's face came into focus—crude and terrifying. I turned on a dime, scrapping my prepared remarks. Instead of showcasing new data on sexual misconduct in Silicon Valley—and the failure of women to rise up the ranks—I told Arianna and that roomful of executives about Sebastian Tyler, the "brilliant jerk" who'd harassed and assaulted me all those years ago, running me out of a dream job and a chosen field. I finished with the following thought: "Looking back through the tunnel of time, what hits me is the enormous age gap. I was just twenty-three, for heaven's sake. He was fifty-two. I didn't stand a chance."

The audience went wild. Some of the female executives hollered and stomped their feet. My face broke into a huge Cheshire cat smile. Along with millions of other women who shared their #MeToo stories that week, I felt exultant, buoyant, and free. It was a wonderful thing to break the silence and slough off decades of shame and self-blame.

My cathartic moment in October of 2017 inspired this book. Beginning that winter I kicked off a new project at CTI (a New York–based research organization that I founded sixteen years ago). The goal was to create a rich stream of qualitative and quantitative research that would give depth and heft to #MeToo and increase the possibility that the movement would drive enduring change.

Little did I know about what I was getting into. For the past two years, I've been on a particularly wild roller coaster, replete with dips and turns and blind corners. Accusations of sexual misconduct, and the fallout of these claims, continued to rumble and roil through our culture—indeed, barely a week passes without new claims and new damage. But despite the proliferation of cases, some days it seems that we've made little progress in figuring out how to deal—consistently and fairly—with either the predators or the prey.

In addition to Harvey Weinstein (the go-to villain of the #MeToo movement) these are just some of the troubling stories that have stood out for me over the last twenty-four months: Google giving a $90 million severance package to Andy Rubin (creator of the Android system) while concealing details of the credible charges of sexual assault that triggered his departure; Terry Crews (a former NFL linebacker and successful actor) winning his sexual assault case against talent agent Adam Venit, only to be attacked by the rapper Curtis "50 Cent" Jackson for failing to fight back "even if that had landed him in jail"; and the recent confirmation (in July 2019) by the Senate of General John Hyten as vice chairman of the Joint Chiefs of Staff despite credible accusations of sexual assault by Army Colonel Kathryn Spletstoser, a widely respected member of his senior staff.

These stories make abundantly clear that #MeToo is still an unfolding story—the roots of the movement and the narrative of how and why it has spread and swelled over the past two and a half years are still being unearthed and investigated. But already there are some clear-cut gains and wins.

The movement has lifted a heavy burden of pain and shame for millions of women; it has spearheaded a huge shift in public opinion, and victims now have a fighting chance of being believed; it has stripped power from a large number of badly behaved men; and it has reinvigorated efforts on the pay equity front and reinforced moves toward inclusive leadership cultures.

Even as we continue to reckon with these complexities, it's critical to seek out new and more rigorous data so as to enable a much more complete understanding of the incidence of sexual and other harassment at work. To some degree, the revelations of the last few years have been particularly shocking and hard to deal with because leaders (businesspeople and politicians alike) had no idea that the problem of sexual misconduct was so widespread and deeply rooted. Many naively assumed that the actions of disgraced moguls like Harvey Weinstein, Roger Ailes, or Jeffrey Epstein were outliers. Now we realize that this assumption is false—abuse can be both extreme and commonplace, and employees have been absorbing this abuse not only from white male bosses but also from others. As my treasure trove of new data shows: a peer can also be a predator. An increasingly number of sexual misconduct cases center on a woman as the predator, and certain sectors and industries are particularly prone to sexual misconduct. For example, the incidence of harassment is literally twice as high in the media as in legal services. The devil really *is* in the details.

One thing this new evidence makes quite clear is that the #MeToo movement has not had a big enough tent: it has not reached beyond the standard story (older white guys hitting on younger white women) to acknowledge, comfort, and support other groups who are also targets of abuse. Think for example of Mahmoud Latif, a gay Muslim man who in December 2018 accused a female supervisor at Morgan Stanley of sexually assaulting him.[1] As we shall see in the pages that follow, men and women of color and LGBTQ employees experience particularly high rates of sexual harassment and assault. Junior, white, straight women are not the only victims, and senior, white, straight men are not the only aggressors.

Another big focus of this book is scoping out the true costs of sexual misconduct. We have come some distance assessing the direct costs—lawsuits and settlements, hits to the brand and to company valuations. But what about the indirect costs? Every revolution has its collateral damage, and this one is no different. In chapter 6, I examine the impact on female progression in particular. As we will see, senior male executives are increasingly skittish about either mentoring or sponsoring junior women, no matter how high-performing they are. Senior men are fearful of gossip and lawsuits. This reaction is having serious knock-on effects, stalling and stunting women's career prospects, and also depriving companies of diversity in the C-suite and "gender smarts" around decision-making tables.

Factoring together indirect and direct costs allows a more complete accounting of the true cost of a sexual scandal, and underscores the fact that the financial hit is always serious and ranges from dire to devastating—think Nike, CBS, Wyn Resorts, Michigan State University, and the Catholic Church.

Given this damage, both to individuals and organizations, it's become a business imperative for leaders to create work environments where everyone—female and male, black and white, gay and straight—can safely and effectively work together across lines of hierarchy and rise according to their merits. Employees (junior as well as senior) also need to take steps to protect themselves and those around them. That's why after analyzing carefully the new CTI data and conducting eighty-plus in-person interviews with those whose lives and enterprises have been upended by sexual misconduct, I've developed an action agenda: a three-pronged strategy that combines legal remedies with individual action steps and corporate best practices, aimed at helping organizations and individual employees navigate this post-#MeToo world. I dig down into "experiments at the edge" as well as more evolved initiatives.

This final "solutions" section of the book tackles head-on the central question: however loud the chorus of pain, has #MeToo damaged balance sheets and recalibrated risk on a scale necessary to drive enduring change in leadership cultures? We are, after all, going for the jugular: asking the old boys' club/old girls' club to cease and desist, to stop weaponizing sex to maintain their grip on power.

#ME TOO

IN THE CORPORATE WORLD

1

#METOO: WHERE WE'RE COMING FROM—AND GOING

Sexual misconduct in the workplace is as old as the hills. Most of us have experienced, witnessed, or at least heard of its most common expression: an older man preying upon a young woman over whom he has power. Maybe he offers her a shortcut to the top in return for sexual favors. Maybe he tells her she can either please him or lose her job. Even if the threat is not so explicit, it is almost always there: typically the young woman's choices are to comply, be fired, or at best to fend him off and lose all hope of professional advancement.

In 1910, a major newspaper apparently had no hesitation in printing the following joke: A man looks out his office window and sees, in a building across the street, a pretty stenographer sitting in her boss's lap. He telephones the boss to say that he can see everything. So the boss pulls down the shade.[1]

In the early 1960s, Helen Gurley Brown (of *Cosmopolitan* and *Sex and the Single Girl* fame) happily described a "game" called Scuttle that she'd seen in an office she worked at: almost every afternoon, a group of men would pick one of the secretaries, chase her around the office, and take her panties off. Brown saw this game as harmless flirtation. Today, I think most of us would recoil in horror and see such a scenario as a form of sexual abuse—after all, the secretary had no ability to say no. Yet for years this sort of behavior was accepted and seen as a legitimate way for men to bond at work.[2]

In 1964, the United States Congress passed the Civil Rights Act, whose Title VII outlawed discrimination against employees for sex, race, color, national origin, or religion.[3] Title VII did *not* forbid sexual harassment—the term didn't even exist. Its definition had to wait for the scholar and writer Lin Farley, who in the 1970s was director of the Women's Section at Cornell University. Farley and her female students discovered that they all had at least once either been fired or forced to quit because of male colleagues' behavior. They described the experience as "sexual harassment." Farley used the term in public during a New York City Commission on Human Rights hearing in 1975 and discussed it at length in her book *Sexual Shakedown*.

The lawyer Catharine MacKinnon then led the legal effort to define unwanted sexual advances as a form of sex discrimination, arguing that in such cases a male boss was treating a female employee differently from how he would treat a man. She publicized sexual harassment as "a crucial expression" of women's inequality in her 1979 book, *Sexual Harassment of Working Women*.[4]

In the 1970s more and more women entered professions and roles that had for decades been reserved for men. Some men reacted with harassment. "The function of sexual harassment in nontraditional jobs is to keep women out; the function of sexual harassment in the traditional female job sector is to keep women down," Farley wrote. She also showed how sexual harassment connects to wage inequality, making the point that harassment keeps many women from staying in a job long enough to be promoted, "effectively forestall(ing) all hopes of higher wages."[5] Recent research has confirmed that interruptions in work are indeed "penalized by lower subsequent wages."[6] The new kid on the block often has to prove her chops from scratch and re-earn pension, health care, and other benefits.

"NUTTY," "SLUTTY," AND A PUNCH LINE

One might think that with all this new attention major societal changes would kick into gear. But as we all know, #MeToo took off in 2018, not in 1979 or even in 2006—the year when Black civil rights activist Tarana Burke began using the phrase "Me Too" to raise awareness of the pervasiveness of sexual abuse. This forty-year-long delay was a result of deeply seated—and entrenched—male privilege, particularly in the world of work.

Consider Clarence Thomas, President George H. W. Bush's pick for the United States Supreme Court in 1991. Shortly before confirmation hearings began, rumors emerged that Thomas had a habit of sexually harassing his employees. But rumors are faceless. Only one woman dared come forward: Anita Hill, who had worked with Thomas at the Department of Education and at the Equal Employment Opportunity Commission (EEOC)—where, ironically enough, he had been in charge of enforcing laws against discrimination.

Joe Biden, then chair of the Senate Judiciary Committee, authorized an FBI investigation and this all-male, all-white committee reopened hearings. Hill—a soft-spoken African American woman—told these fourteen men that Thomas had spoken to her suggestively about pornographic films depicting large penises or large breasts. He had also bragged to her about his own sexual prowess. The committee responded with anger—against Hill. One senator suggested that her testimony was the "product of fantasy," another that she was merely "a scorned woman."[7] The press was no better. One journalist, David Brock, called Hill—in spite of her unflinchingly professional demeanor—"A little bit nutty and a little bit slutty." Brock even published a book, *The Real Anita Hill*, which smeared her character. Brock later admitted that his "journalism" and his book had been intentional hit jobs on Hill and that some of his sources "admitted to me that they always knew Thomas was guilty as charged . . . Clarence Thomas almost certainly perjured himself to gain his seat."[8]

In Brock's opinion, something similar happened in 2018, when Christine Blasey Ford accused another Supreme Court nominee, Brett Kavanaugh, of having sexually assaulted her. Brock wrote that "Kavanaugh's categorical denial of Ford's account is not credible . . . people need to see through all the Republican smoke and take his protestations with a heavy grain of salt." Public outrage, Blasey Ford's credible testimony, and the presence of four women on the Senate Judiciary Committee were not enough to disqualify Kavanaugh. The Senate voted—50 to 48—to confirm his appointment to the nation's highest court where not only his legal philosophy but also his ethical and moral stances will help determine cases for years to come.

The #MeToo movement will have to become much more inclusive itself. A few years after Thomas joined the Supreme Court, a so-called affair between the most powerful man in the world and a naive twenty-two-year-old intern also made headlines. Strictly speaking, the case of Bill Clinton and Monica Lewinsky resides in a gray zone, since although many people considered his behavior sexual misconduct, it was not harassment or assault. By Lewinsky's own account, she began the flirtation with the president of the United States, then forty-eight years old and married, and she consented to their sexual relationship.[9] Yet Lewinsky later admitted that she had only "a limited understanding of the consequences . . . I now see how problematic it was that the two of us even got to a place where there was a question of consent. Instead, the road that led there was littered with inappropriate abuse of authority, station, and privilege."[10]

As the data will show in chapter 2, even consensual relationships, *if* they cross hierarchal lines, create problems both for the individuals involved and the organizations where they work. But more salient to the history of #MeToo is that this "affair" renewed interest in President Clinton's long history of sexual misconduct, including multiple accusations of harassment, abuse of power over women who worked for him, and at least one credible accusation of rape.[11]

Yet this publicity did *not* lead to a #MeToo moment. On the contrary, Clinton survived impeachment and went on to have a distinguished post-presidential career as a philanthropist, author, and statesman—while Lewinsky became a global punch line.[12] Branded by this incident, she had trouble finding a job for two decades.[13] Only in recent years has she found a niche as an anti-cyberbullying advocate and a contributing writer to *Vanity Fair*, which gives her a platform to, at last, speak as a warrior in the #MeToo movement.

The experiences of Lewinsky and Hill demonstrate that for thirty years after Title VII of the Civil Rights Act became law, not much changed. Predators faced little or no consequence for harassing or assaulting those in their power. While victims faced ridicule, damaged careers, and even organized smear campaigns.

BREAKING THROUGH:
ASHLEY JUDD, GWYNETH PALTROW, AND
EIGHTY-FIVE OTHERS

What finally forced organizations and the wider public to ac-knowledge sexual harassment and assault as the crisis that it is? The shift didn't happen overnight; rather it resembled a slow burn, as a series of scandals pierced the nation's conscience and rubbed the noses of millions of victims into their pain.

The first breakthrough scandal hit the headlines in 2002, when the *Boston Globe* ran a well-researched piece on Catholic priests molesting children. Each year since has brought to light further instances of sexual assault inside the Church, where men in power apparently felt free, protected by top leadership, to abuse and rape children. Catholic priests were not the only authority figures that saw their reputations collapse as their misconduct became known. For millions of Americans, Bill Cosby had once repre-sented a kindly father figure, yet dozens of women came forward to accuse him, amid much media attention, of assault. Fox News chairman Roger Ailes and top-rated anchor Bill O'Reilly also drew attention—and finally widespread condemnation—for their sexual misconduct at their company.

Another turning point in public opinion was the election of Donald Trump to the presidency of the United States in the fall of 2016. Many people remember the *Access Hollywood* video tape where candidate Trump boasted to television host Billy Bush of groping women: "You know I'm automatically attracted to beautiful women. I just start kissing them . . . And when you're a star they let you do it. You can do anything. Grab them by the p***y." The election of a man openly proud of being a groper infuriated many women (and men) who had suffered or witnessed such behavior.

As the *New York Times* journalists who covered much of the beginning of the #MeToo movement said in an interview with *Variety*, after the election of Donald Trump many women "felt angered and empowered to come forward."[14]

Yet if all these incidents involving powerful institutions and men lit the fuse, it was a Hollywood producer who set off the explosion. The casting couch has long been a place where women have suffered harassment and assault—with little or no legal protection. Most actresses are free agents, who therefore do not enjoy the protections of Title VII of the Civil Rights Act.[15] But when enough famous victims come forward, and when the behavior is egregious enough to command horrified attention all over the world, it's just not possible to ignore their claims against a powerful predator. It is also possible for a movement to begin.

In October 2017, the *New York Times* broke the story that movie mogul Harvey Weinstein was a serial sexual assailant. Within a few months, the list of women accusing him of misconduct grew to eighty-seven: he had raped multiple actresses vaginally and orally, grabbed a young girl's breasts and forced his hands up her skirt during a work meeting in his New York office, ruined multiple actresses' careers when they refused sex with him, masturbated in front of girls as young as eighteen, ordered others to strip for him on movie sets, threatened to kill one actress for refusing him, got naked and chased other women around the studio, held a woman by the neck while he masturbated in front of her with his other hand, and on and on.[16] And it wasn't just actresses whom he preyed upon: female employees of the Weinstein Company talked among themselves about his behavior and would double up for protection when they met with him.[17]

The sheer number of victims, as well as the fact that some of them—such as Gwyneth Paltrow, Ashley Judd, and Angelina Jolie—

were world-famous *and* willing to publicly come forward was enough, finally: the #MeToo movement began, encouraging first women, then men, too, to break the silence and shame that previously haunted the *victims* of sexual misconduct.

It was a long road, starting with the Civil Rights Act in 1964 and feminist scholars and activists in the 1970s, passing through scandals involving a Supreme Court nominee and a president in the 1990s, taking in hard-hitting press coverage of abuse in the Catholic Church and among celebrities in the 2000s, encompassing a howl of pain among many women when yet another sexual predator won election as president in 2016, until finally the sheer undeniable horror of Harvey Weinstein—and the fame and number of his victims—broke through the dam of silence and shame.

THE FLOODGATES HAVE OPENED—
FOR GOOD

I read the *New York Times* every day, and here is what I came across during a perfectly normal week in March 2019. On a Monday, this headline appeared: "Google Approved $45 Million Exit Package for Executive Accused of Misconduct." As the result of a shareholder lawsuit, the article explained, Google had to reveal that, in 2016, rather than firing for cause a top executive who had groped a subordinate, the company paid him a cool $45 million to leave quietly. The same article also mentioned a $90 million exit package given to another Google executive credibly accused of sexual misconduct.[18] Anyone who thinks that crime doesn't pay clearly should think again; sexual harassment and assault can be extremely lucrative!

Friday that same week, I opened the business section of the

Times to see this headline: "It's the Biggest #MeToo Case on Wall Street, and Someone Is Lying." The lead article told the story of Sara Tirschwell, a senior executive at an asset manager who accused her boss of having pressured her into sex—and accused her company of firing her when she complained. Both her boss and the company deny her allegation, but discovery is now under way on her $30 million lawsuit.[19]

Two days later, once again on the front page of the business section of the *New York Times*, I saw this headline: "Women in Economics Report Rampant Sexual Assault and Bias." According to the American Economic Association, the article reported, one hundred female economists claim that a peer or colleague has sexually assaulted them. One in five claim they had been subjected to unwanted sexual advances. Indeed, fully half of the women who responded to the survey said they had been treated unfairly because of their gender.[20] (This piece hit me in the gut, bringing back memories of how Sebastian's abuse had wrecked my first career. As an economist by training I can very much relate to the pain of these women.)

What do these three articles, in a single newspaper in a single week, indicate? To me, these articles—which describe predatory behavior that spans years, if not decades—demonstrate that more than two years after Harvey Weinstein's crimes revved up #MeToo and put it on the front burner (it's important to note that Weinstein didn't "invent" #MeToo, activist Tarana Burke coined this term as early as 2006), the movement is still going strong. It is bringing incidents to light that organizations had thought they could sweep under the rug, giving victims a chance at recourse, and pressuring companies and institutions—none of which, surely, want to be the target of a $30 million lawsuit or a negative headline in the *New York Times*—to change their ways.

#MeToo has not ended. On the contrary, we may not even yet be at the end of the beginning. Yet already there is much good news, as well as bad news, from the #MeToo front—and a great deal of on-going momentum.

GOOD NEWS

The Silence Has Been Broken

Aside from the continuing bravery of victims (such as those listed previously) coming forward each day and the consistent (if belated) attention of the media and the courts to their stories, I'd like to call out that *institutions* are also abandoning their prior code of silence, or rather, their code of "pay everyone to keep it quiet." In February 2019, for example, the director of the National Institutes of Health (NIH) issued a formal apology to women in STEM. "The reports of scientists and students shared through the #MeTooSTEM movement portray a heartbreaking story of opportunities lost, pain suffered, and a systemic failure to protect and defend," the statement said. "To all those who have endured these experiences, we are sorry that it has taken so long to acknowledge and address the climate and culture that has caused such harm."[21]

Norms and Attitudes Are Shifting

Five years ago, two thirds of Americans said that a woman who reported being sexually harassed was risking her career. Today, in a sign that #MeToo has made it safer for victims to speak up, now less than half say the same. Today most Americans *believe* the victims—83 percent of women say that those who report being victims of sexual assault should be given the benefit of the doubt, as do 72 percent of men.[22]

In the year following the revelation of Harvey Weinstein's sexual predations and the start of #MeToo, at least 201 prominent men lost jobs or major roles. Fifty-four of their replacements are women.[23] As we will explore in chapters 3 and 4, women, too, can be predators and men can be victims, but there has clearly been a change in how companies weigh the risks of putting a man or woman in a top job. As Joan Williams, a law professor at the University of California, Hastings, said, "Women have always been seen as risky, because they might do something like have a baby. But men are now being seen as more risky hires."[24]

Jennifer Salke, who became chief of programming at Amazon Studios after accusations of sexual harassment ousted a man, talked about the change in attitudes that a woman at the top brings. "I had two or three weeks of executives and people across the company on my sofa, many of them women, talking about their experiences and how they were feeling and wanting [me] to be someone who could listen and be an advocate for them," she said.[25] One of the first problems Salke had to handle was a Woody Allen movie that Amazon had agreed to distribute, *A Rainy Day in New York*. Industry insiders were calling it "toxic" after "renewed attention to the sexual molestation allegations leveled at the filmmaker by his daughter Dylan Farrow." Salke made the tough decision to terminate the new movie and three additional deals for future pictures with Allen.[26]

At the Sundance Film Festival in January 2019, Time's Up and the Annenberg Inclusion Initiative presented the entertainment industry with the Four Percent Challenge, urging studios and top actors to work on a feature film with a woman director. Of 1,200 films made between 2007 and 2018, women directed only

4 percent.[27] This challenge, if accepted, could further accelerate a change in societal attitudes. "None of us in this room have grown up or seen a film with fully realized female characters," Dr. Stacy L. Smith, founder and director of the Annenberg Inclusion Initiative, said in a TED Talk. "What would happen if the next generation of audiences grew up with a whole new screen reality?"[28]

Companies Are Coming Clean

In one fiscal year alone, Fox News incurred $50 million in legal costs due to sexual misconduct among its executives.[29] As I'll explore in chapter 6, the legal and reputational risks to companies have grown enormous, in part thanks to #MeToo. Perhaps because nothing focuses a corporate leader's attention quite so well as the threat of losing tens of millions of dollars, more and more companies are breaking the silence about misconduct in their ranks. Many are even making good faith efforts to clean things up.

When credible accusations of sexual misconduct emerged at professional services firm Deloitte UK, its CEO David Sproul decided to confront the problem head-on. Women were initially skeptical that anyone would pay attention to misconduct at one of the Big Four accounting firms. "Who cares that Senior VP Andrew McCormick grabbed my boobs and tried to kiss me in a drunken rage at a bar? It will not start his downfall similar to the Weinsteins and Spaceys of this world," one woman from Deloitte US posted on Reddit.[30]

That woman was wrong. Sproul took action and then released figures to boost transparency: as of December 2018, the firm revealed, approximately twenty partners had been fired for sexual misconduct. PwC, EY, and KPMG's UK operations soon followed with similar firings and at least some transparency.[31] Other forward-thinking companies are also taking action to make workplaces—and balance sheets—safe from the damage that sexual misconduct can cause, as this book's last chapter will describe.

Investors Are Paying Attention

An anonymous group of shareholders filed suit against Nike in September 2018, citing sexual harassment and gender discrimination claims inside the sportswear giant. The lawsuit alleged that a hostile work environment has harmed "and threatens to further tarnish and impair" the company's "financial position, as well as its reputation and goodwill."[32] The investment firm Trillium Asset Management also took action, filing a first-ever proposal on sexual misconduct risk management. The proposal asked Nike to consider linking executive compensation performance metrics to improvements in corporate culture and diversity, though Trillium withdrew it after the sportswear titan agreed to an ongoing dialogue on the topic.[33]

Another group of shareholders is suing the board of directors of Google's parent company, Alphabet, over a $90 million exit package given to a man credibly accused of sexual misconduct, Andy Rubin.[34] In addition the California Public Employees' Retirement System (CalPERS) and other California pension funds are considering demanding of investees that all sexual harassment settlements, including those involving top leaders, be reported to the company's board, and that settlements of a material size be publicly disclosed.[35]

Thanks to #MeToo, investors are increasingly aware that sexual misconduct is a serious business risk.

#MeToo Is Spreading into the Blue-Collar Workforce

Even if #MeToo began in Hollywood, and women in well-paid professions such as media and technology have grabbed most of the attention, sexual misconduct clearly haunts blue-collar work-places, too—and women there are speaking up and suing. The Center for American Progress has found, based on data from the EEOC, endemic sexual harassment in the hospitality sector and in retail.[36] In the restaurant trade, where servers are frequently at the mercy of both managers and clients, another study found that 30 percent of women and 20 percent of men reported that "inap-propriate touching" was a "common occurrence."[37]

Now, thanks to #MeToo, such workers are more likely to speak up when they suffer sexual harassment or assault—and they increasingly have the means to make corporate leaders pay attention. Workers at McDonald's, for example, have launched protests and filed lawsuits, backed by a $25 million legal defense fund created to extend #MeToo into the blue-collar workforce. McDonald's has already taken some measures in response, includ-ing training for frontline employees and a complaint hotline.[38]

NOT-SO-GOOD NEWS

The Boomerang Boys

Do consequences endure? Do the punishments meted out to high-profile sexual predators significantly limit their careers? The jury is still out on this question in the era of #MeToo but it seems disturbingly possible that very little has changed: a few slaps on the wrist and then it's back to business as usual.

Charlie Rose, forced to resign his job as a TV talk show host over misconduct, has pitched a new talk show: interviewing other men who have lost their jobs due to sexual misconduct. (Perhaps

Charlie Rose has at least now given the world a new definition for *chutzpah*.) Louis C.K. did at least initially take a small stab at an apology toward the women he had harassed. But he has since returned to the stand-up comedy circuit and made a point of *not* expressing remorse in his routines. Former Google executive Andy Rubin not only received a $90 million exit package; Google has also invested millions more in his new business venture. Emil Michael, once an instrumental dealmaker for Uber's founder, had to quit after a torrent of misconduct. After a year off, the hedge fund firm Coatue Management hired him as a consultant.[39]

And the man whose misconduct single-handedly launched #MeToo as a worldwide movement, Harvey Weinstein? He lost his company and his reputation, true, but a group of accusers who had filed civil suits against him were "heartbroken," as one put it, when they learned in June 2019 that they were likely to get a settlement totaling $44 million, which was less than half of what they'd originally expected to receive. At this writing the proposed deal was uncertain anyway because of a dispute between the Weinstein Co. estate and former company directors who have been accused of enabling his conduct. It's also true that lawyers for the victims have said that the terms would allow Weinstein and the directors to escape liability and accountability, without "contributing a dime of their own money!"[40]

As I'll discuss in chapter 9, an accusation should not be an instant condemnation; some organizations, such as IBM, have found effective ways to both clamp down on false accusations and enable offenders to earn forgiveness and redemption. But it is disturbing to see so many serious serial offenders pass through a brief "wilderness" then bounce right back.

Skittish Senior Men

What to do if you're a senior man who has seen other senior men brought down by women accusing them of sexual misconduct? A sensible answer would be: treat all your reports, women and men, with respect, while taking a few straightforward steps (which I outline in chapter 8) to avoid any risk of malicious gossip or misunderstandings.

But another, distressingly common answer—akin to amputating one's arm from fear of breaking it—is to avoid women at work altogether. Hiring a woman has become "an unknown risk," a senior wealth manager said in an article on the "Pence Effect" on Wall Street.[41] The label comes from US Vice President Mike Pence, who famously avoids having a meal alone with any woman other than his wife. It is depressing that Mr. Pence sees women primarily as vessels of temptation, whom his flesh is too weak to resist. It is also highly unjust to women in his field, who will not be able to form professional bonds over meals with this powerful man as their male colleagues can.

Tragically, #MeToo backlash is part of the reason why more and more men have grown nervous about sponsoring, hiring, or even meeting one-on-one with a woman. CTI's study found that about two in five men and women agreed that "recent publicity about sexual harassment at work makes it even less likely that a male leader will sponsor a female protégée even if she deserves it."[42]

The Legal Backlash

Some men credibly accused of sexual predation are fighting back in court. Following Salke's decision to pull Amazon out of its deal to distribute Woody Allen's movies—in which Amazon cited "renewed allegations against Mr. Allen, his own controversial comments, and the increasing refusal of top talent to work with or be associated with him in any way"—Allen is suing Amazon for $68 million.[43] Similarly, after advertising agency McCann Health fired its global chief creative officer Jeremy Perrott over sexual harassment allegations, Perrott is suing for $25 million in damages.[44] Such legal cases both complicate and increase the risks for companies with sexual predators in their ranks, who may have to face lawsuits from two sides: from the predators' victims and from the predators themselves. It's yet another reason why it is critical to create a workplace environment where predators cannot thrive— as I'll describe in this book's second part.

"One Free Grope"

Title VII of the 1964 Civil Rights Act was a positive step, which lawyers have managed to apply to many cases of sexual harassment and assault. But as a legal instrument, it has its limitations. It only applies to companies with fifteen or more employees, and excludes from its protection independent contractors—such as the actresses whom Harvey Weinstein abused. In addition its statute of limitations for filing a claim is only 180 days, or 300 days if there's a corresponding state law. Some states are now addressing these and other shortcomings in the federal law with more stringent laws of their own (see chapter 7).

In 1986, the Supreme Court unanimously ruled that unwelcome sexual advances, which create an offensive working environment, violate Title VII. However, the court said, the harassment must be "sufficiently severe or pervasive to alter the conditions of . . . employment and create an abusive working environment."[45] That's often a high bar to clear. In one infamous instance, the United States Court of Appeals for the Ninth Circuit ruled that a supervisor forcefully groping the breasts of an employee while she was working, boxing her in with his body so that she could not escape, wasn't a severe enough offense to qualify as illegal harassment, since it occurred only once.[46] The case, Brooks v. San Mateo, has become known in legal circles as the "one free grope" rule.

All in all, as Gillian Thomas of the ACLU puts it, "Sexual harassment has been illegal for more than forty years, but there have been some pretty clear instances of sexual harassment that the courts didn't see as illegal." Yet since the 1970s employers have been addressing sexual misconduct based narrowly on the law, protecting themselves with "training programs" that are often lipstick on a pig. Lawyers hired by CBS's board to investigate then CEO Les Moonves found that senior people in the news division generally had their assistants complete the training for them.[47]

Other rulings have also made legal recourse difficult for victims. In *Vance v. Ball State University* in 2013, the Supreme Court ruled that an employer is not liable for an offender's misconduct unless the offender is a *direct* supervisor of the plaintiff. (Unsurprisingly, defendants have found ways to fashion highly flexible definitions of "direct supervisor.")

In *University of Texas Southwestern Medical Center v. Nassar* in 2013, the court ruled that a victim accusing her employer or supervisor of retaliating against her for complaining must prove that retaliation was the *sole* motive for having fired or transferred the victim. Since it's impossible to read minds, it's hard to prove a supervisor's sole motivation. Practically speaking, if a victim ever showed up late for a meeting or fell a little short on a performance metric, as everyone does now and then, the employer can cite such occurrences and escape liability. This escape valve is a serious impediment to to the entire possibility of legal redress, since so many victims of sexual harassment and assault are *punished* by their companies when they complain. In 2018, the EEOC received 39,469 complaints alleging such retaliation.[48]

Well-intentioned leaders are sometimes surprised to find that misconduct has gone unreported—because the victims feared reprisal. "We've seen cases where three quarters of employees who've experienced sexual misconduct at their company don't report incidents because they fear retaliation," says Pooja Jain-Link, an executive vice president and the head of research at CTI.

Now, in part thanks to #MeToo, the legal scenario for companies is changing, raising both hope for victims and the risks for companies, as I'll explore later in this book.

REAL CHANGE

Fear of lawsuits may be a necessary starting point for some companies and leaders, but real change requires more than damage control. Individuals can and must act, but given the scale of the sexual misconduct problem, companies need to get heavily involved. This is an inflection point in our society and organizations need to take a long hard look at their cultures and make a much more vigorous commitment to core values, such as respect for others and equality of treatment. Simultaneously, they must seriously invest in rigorous programs that drive inclusion. Ridding hiring and promotion systems of bias and fear is a good beginning, but as we shall see in later chapters of this book, there is much that corporations and institutions can do—indeed many are already doing.

Brande Stellings, founder of Vestry Laight and a former head of advisory services at Catalyst, notes that the #MeToo movement has helped many C-level executives "recognize that preventing sexual misconduct should be part of a larger conversation about company values and the 'wins' associated with inclusion." That larger conversation—which I'll show how to create and drive in chapters 8 and 9—can avoid the backlash against #MeToo: men feeling resentful and "got at" rather than eager to be part of the solution. "A lot of the gray areas would be less gray if people had more conversations about values and value," Stelling says.

Yet, however insightful, conversations can easily become useless exercises unless they're grounded in hard data. In the next chapter we'll look at the results of CTI's nationally represented survey of sexual misconduct among white-collar workers in the United States and examine the impact of misconduct on individuals and the organizations where they work. This survey allows a much more precise measurement of the problem's scope and span than has been available to date. As we shall see, one key takeaway is that, to truly drive change, the #MeToo movement will have to become much more inclusive itself.

WHAT THE NUMBERS TELL US

2

MEASURING AND MAPPING

Everyone reading this book surely knows that sexual misconduct haunts the corporate world. It's in the headlines every week. But before we can fight the problem, we need to map out—in concrete detail—its scope and span. Here are some of the specific questions about sexual misconduct in the workplace that anyone concerned—whether in leadership or the ranks—needs to be able to answer, to protect themselves and their organizations:

- How common is it?
- How often is it harassment, and how often assault?
- Who are the predators?
- Who are the prey?
- Are certain ethnic groups or LGBTQ individuals especially at risk?
- How closely related is sexual misconduct to seniority and abuse of power?
- How often are harassment and assault reported—and how often ignored?
- How does it impact employee engagement and flight risk—including for bystanders?
- Are consensual sexual relationships in the workplace a problem, too?

- How does workplace sexual misconduct impact women's professional opportunities?
- In what sectors and industries is the problem most severe?

To find out the answers, in 2018 the Center for Talent Innovation, a New York–based think tank that I founded, fielded a nationally representative survey of 3,213 college-educated employees between the ages of twenty-one and sixty-five currently working in full-time white-collar jobs.

Some of the results are surprising.

HARASSMENT VS ASSAULT

Neither is ever acceptable, but there is a difference between sexual harassment (unwanted sexual advances) and assault (unwanted sexual contact). Both terms are broad. Harassment may include anything from inappropriate e-mails to stalking, while assault ranges from groping to rape. Still, the terms do serve as a shorthand for two different degrees of misconduct.

Employees who have been sexually harassed at work

34% of female employees   **13%** of male employees

Harassment is appallingly common: more than one third of women report having been harassed in the workplace at some point in their careers. The vast majority of these women have been harassed by a man (97 percent). Yet some may find it surprising that 13 percent of men also report having suffered sexual harassment. I'll dive deeper into this finding a little later.

Sexual assault is much rarer, but still disturbingly common. If you are in a company with one hundred men and one hundred women, odds are that seven of your female coworkers and five of your male coworkers have suffered physical, sexual assault in the workplace.

Employees who have been sexually **assaulted** at work

7% of female employees   **5%** of male employees

WOMEN AS PREDATORS

Most of us, when we think of sexual harassment and assault, we assume that it is a man abusing his power over a woman. We are usually right to think of sexual misconduct in the workplace that way: as the data shows, it's the most common scenario—but it's not the only one.

When employees have been sexually **harassed**, here's what they say about the **gender** of the perpetrator(s)

Women who have been sexually harassed by...   Men who have been sexually harassed by...

Women: 13%   **Women: 68%**

Men: 97%   **Men: 57%**

The data tells us that 97 percent of women who suffer harassment have been harassed by a man. However, an additional 13 percent have been harassed by another woman. (The numbers add up to more than 100 percent because a subset of women suffered workplace harassment from both a man and a woman at some point in their careers.) In addition, in the much smaller pool of men who suffer harassment, 68 percent say they have been harassed by a woman.

As we shall see in chapters 3 and 4, even more than sexual desire, power (and the desire to acquire or hang on to the perks of power) appears to be the dominant factor underlying most workplace sexual misconduct.

MEN AS PREY

As I noted earlier, more than one in eight men has suffered sexual harassment in the workplace, and one in twenty has suffered assault. This data on the gender of the perpetrator is surprising, particularly with regard to sexual assault. Among the small group of white-collar male employees who experience sexual assault, it's twice as common (76 percent) for men to report assault by a woman than by another man (38 percent). The perpetrators of harassment of men are more evenly divided, but women are still more commonly cited: 68 percent vs 57 percent.

When employees have been sexually **assaulted**, here's what they say about the **gender** of the perpetrator(s)

Women who have been sexually assaulted by...

Women: 19%
Men: 94%

Men who have been sexually assaulted by...

Women: 76%
Men: 38%

It's hard to wrap one's mind around this data, since it goes against the stereotype (perpetrators are supposed to be male and victims are supposed to be female), yet the fact remains that when a man suffers harassment and assault in the workplace, the predator is more likely to be a woman than a man. This underlies a recurring theme in this book: the dynamics at play in workplace sexual misconduct cases have less to do with lust or superior physical force than with ruthless power plays.

If your boss, with power over your career, gropes you or insists on a late-night hotel room visit, you may be afraid to say no or file a complaint, regardless of whether that boss is a man or a woman.

SEXUAL ORIENTATION AND RACE

LGBTQ individuals and people of color are often seen as lower on the societal totem pole than Caucasian straight people. It's therefore not surprising (though still appalling) that these cohorts are especially likely to experience sexual abuse at work. Remember that #MeToo was kicked off by a Black woman: Tarana Burke, a civil rights activist from the Bronx, started the nascent movement in 2006.

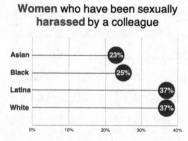

Women who have been sexually **harassed** by a colleague

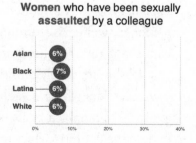

Women who have been sexually **assaulted** by a colleague

Latina women report particularly high levels of sexual harassment (37 percent). As we shall see in chapter 5, male supervisors tend to see them as "hot" and available. When it comes to sexual assault, Black women are especially targeted, but they are not alone in being singled out: their "brothers" are also preyed upon disproportionately. The figures are alarming: fully 21 percent of African American male employees experience sexual harassment (compared to 13 percent of all men) and 7 percent experience sexual assault (compared to 4 percent of white men). As I will discuss in chapter 5, black men are hit upon not only because they are seen as vulnerable and exploitable but also because they are seen as objects of desire and are fetishized by at least some female colleagues. This is an example of the complexity—and ugliness—of sexual misconduct at work.

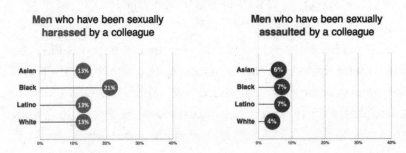

Turning to sexual orientation, the data is equally distressing and some of the figures are startling. LGBTQ employees are more likely to be harassed and assaulted than *any* other groups. Indeed, the figure for gay women is stunningly high (43 percent say they have been harassed, a number that is much higher than women in general). I will delve more deeply into this data in chapter 5, though I wish to underscore now that research in this area is only just getting off the ground. I'm humbled by its complexity and realize I cannot pretend to have the definitive story on the experience of people of color and LGBTQ employees with sexual harassment and assault.

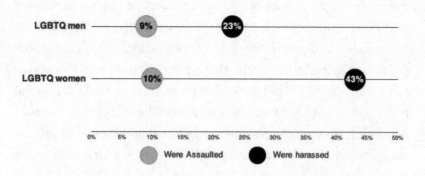

SEXUAL MISCONDUCT AND SENIORITY

In this world of sexual misconduct, how often is the predator more senior (in terms of rank) than their prey? The short answer is often, but not always, especially when the victim is a man or a person of color.

Seventy percent of women who say they have been harassed at work say they were harassed by a senior colleague. The figure for men is lower (59 percent). Indeed, 22 percent of men who have suffered harassment say they were harassed by a colleague *junior* to them. The figure for women is significantly lower (16 percent).

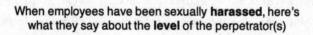

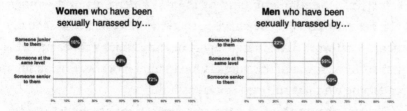

Turning to assault, there are fewer gender differences. A high percentage of both women and men who have been assaulted say they were assaulted by a colleague at the same level of seniority in the organization. (Once again, the numbers add up to more than 100 percent, since some employees report suffering assault from colleagues at different levels in the organization.) The data on men seems to contradict my thesis that power relations underlie sexual misconduct in the workplace. But given how many LGBTQ and black men suffer harassment and assault (see page 27), I would argue that these numbers reflect the fact that societal hierarchies surrounding sexual orientation and race matter as much as work-place hierarchies.

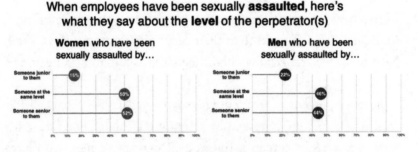

When employees have been sexually assaulted, here's what they say about the level of the perpetrator(s)

Women who have been sexually assaulted by...

Someone junior to them — 15%
Someone at the same level — 50%
Someone senior to them — 52%

Men who have been sexually assaulted by...

Someone junior to them — 22%
Someone at the same level — 46%
Someone senior to them — 44%

SECONDHAND SMOKE

Those who witness others suffering sexual harassment and assault in the workplace tend to speak up—just not very loudly or effectively. Similar numbers of men (12 percent) and women (13 percent) say that they have witnessed someone being sexually harassed at work. One in five report hearing about a colleague who has suffered sexual harassment. One in ten report hearing about a colleague who has suffered sexual assault.

Yet less than a third of witnesses *report* the misconduct to HR. Roughly a third of witnesses speak up in the moment, and more vent to family and friends (on the venting front, women do a much better job than men). On the reporting front, women do slightly bet-

ter than men, with 30 percent of female witnesses reporting to HR
compared to 23 percent of male witnesses. This is where the rubber
hits the road: without a formal complaint the odds of organizational
action are minimal. Of course, as we'll see in later chapters, even
with a formal complaint, organizational action is rare. In fact, given
the specter of retaliation, in many organizations, it may be tragic—
but logical—for witnesses, like the victims themselves, to keep quiet.

When employees have witnessed someone being sexually harassed by a colleague, here's how they responded

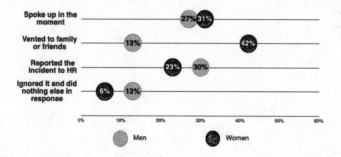

For many years in corporate America, it has been worse to be
a "troublemaker," spitefully squealing about a star performer's
predatory behavior, than a star performer with a habit of raping
underlings. Harassment and assault, in other words, create "secondhand smoke": a toxic atmosphere that makes witnesses fearful or
hesitant to do the right thing.

DISENGAGEMENT AND FLIGHT RISK

When employees witness harassment and assault it impacts morale and engagement. It's only logical: if you see the boss harassing

or assaulting a colleague and then geting away with it, it's hard for you to believe that you are working in a safe, respectful environment where everyone is assessed on the value they bring to the table.

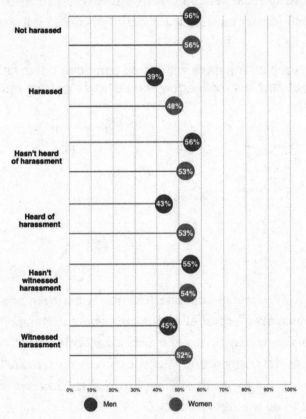

Employees who are satisfied with their current job

Naturally, given the personal trauma involved, those who suffer harassment or assault take an even bigger hit to morale, engagement, and job satisfaction in general. Interestingly, women report a smaller hit to job satisfaction than men, whether they suffer harassment or merely witness it. Men's job satisfaction falls to 39 percent from 56 percent when they suffer harassment, while women's satisfaction falls "only" to 48 percent from 56 percent. For men who witness harassment, job satisfaction falls to 46 percent, while women's job satisfaction is essentially unchanged. Why this gender disparity?

I will hazard a guess: women are more used to both suffering sexual harassment and seeing it in the workplace, so many may tragically accept it as a fact of life. But with the rekindling of awareness and outrage that #MeToo has brought, I believe that this resignation will become much less common going forward. As we'll see in chapter 7, the courts' tolerance of sexual misconduct is most definitely declining.

CONSENSUAL RELATIONSHIPS CAN BE TOXIC, TOO

Most workplaces are full of empowered individuals (consenting adults) who have much in common with one another. It is therefore natural (and thoroughly acceptable) to look for and perhaps find a mate at work. But when sexual relationships intersect with workplace power dynamics, problems emerge. In an earlier CTI study, published by *Harvard Business Review*,[1] we asked white-collar workers about affairs between junior and senior team members.

We found that they are a) common and b) roundly condemned. Eleven percent of employees said that they knew of someone on their team who had a sexual relationship with a boss or supervisor. Seventy-one percent of employees said that they found these relationships inappropriate.

The reasons for this disapproval aren't ideological. They're pragmatic. Here's why:

- **Morale takes a hit.** Twenty-five percent reported a falloff in dedication and commitment on the team when a boss or supervisor was sleeping with a subordinate.
- **Respect takes a hit.** Twenty-two percent said the team lost respect for the boss or supervisor involved, and another 17 percent said the team lost respect for the boss's lover.
- **Performance and productivity suffer.** Fourteen percent reported that team performance deteriorated when the boss was sleeping with a subordinate, and 11 percent reported that team productivity declined.

Effects of a boss-subordinate affair, as perceived by their teams

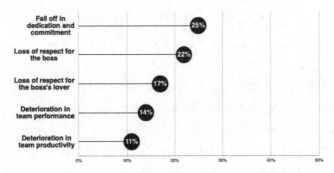

IMPACT ON SPONSORSHIP AND PROGRESSION

It's one of the most important pieces of collateral damage from #MeToo: women, already at a disadvantage when it came to winning a senior person's support to boost them up the corporate ladder, may now be even *more* disadvantaged. Nearly two out of five women agree with the statement that "recent publicity about sexual harassment at work makes it even less likely that a male leader will sponsor a female protégé—even if she deserves it."

In my earlier book, *Forget a Mentor, Find a Sponsor*, I quantified the value to protégés of winning a sponsor: female employees with a sponsor are 19 percent more likely to get that next promotion than those without. (For male employees the figure is 20 percent.) Meaning that when men refuse to sponsor high-performing women, from fear of gossip or scandal, they are denying women opportunities that their male peers enjoy. In a world where a shortage of women around decision-making tables is a drag on innovation and new market growth (see discussion in chapters 6 and 9), this is the last thing companies need.

WHERE THE PROBLEM IS MOST SEVERE

What's the worst occupation or sector, if you're looking place for an environment free of harassment and assault? The answer is media

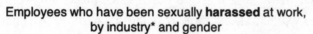

Employees who have been sexually harassed at work, by industry* and gender

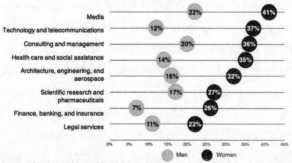

*Media includes art and design services, public relations/ advertising services, video and audio production and broadcasting, entertainment, publishing, and other communications.
Business/ Consulting includes management, business Consulting services, business operations, and small business.
Scientific research and pharma includes life, physical, and social scientific research, and development and pharma.

(with technology coming in second). In the media industry a full 41 percent of women and 22 percent of men report harassment. It's much better (or at least safer) to work in finance or legal services.

Digging a little deeper, the data is surprising. Who knew that men are much safer in technology than in media! (Though both sectors are off the charts in terms of the harassment of women.) And it's a pleasant shock that finance is relatively tame these days. After all, the banking and hedge fund world has provided rich material on sexual harassment and assault for a number of high-profile movies (such as *The Wolf of Wall Street*) and lawsuits.

To take just two famous examples, Martens v. Smith Barney (over sex discrimination, sexual harassment, and retaliation, including the infamous "boom-boom room") led to a $150 million payout,[2] while Ingraham v. UBS led to a $10 million award to a woman who was repeatedly humiliated by requests for sex, comments on her body, and instructions to perform oral sex on a client.[3] As a *Wall Street Journal* reporter at the time put it, women on Wall Street in the 1980s didn't call it sexual harassment. "We called it going to work."[4] Given that history, it may seem surprising that financial firms appear to be much safer places for women (and men) to work than technology or health care. As we shall see in this book's last section, Wall Street has done a relatively good job in mitigating the top risk factors (see sidebar on the next page), so that potential predators cannot act with impunity.

In later chapters, I'll explain these findings, as well as the other surprising results from CTI's survey—and then provide a way forward, both for individuals and organizations. But first, in the next three chapters, I'll look at the data on rarely discussed kinds of sexual misconduct: when the targets are not young white women, but other vulnerable groups in the white-collar workforce.

Top Risk Factors for Sexual Misconduct

The EEOC says an organization is most likely to have a sexual misconduct problem if one or more of these conditions exist:

- A homogenous workforce
- A workplace where some workers do not conform to workplace norms
- Cultural and language differences in the workplace
- Coarsened social discourse outside the workplace
- A workforce with many young workers
- A workplace with many teenagers and young adults
- A workplace with "high value" employees
- A workplace with significant power disparities
- A workplace that relies on customer service or client satisfaction
- A workplace where work is monotonous or consists of low-intensity tasks
- Isolated workspaces
- Workplace cultures that tolerate or encourage alcohol consumption
- A decentralized workplace[5]

3

WOMEN AS PREDATORS

The professor had a habit of addressing a certain graduate student in e-mails as "my most adored one" and "sweet cuddly baby." The messages were full of the professor's fantasies: "My image during meditation: we're on the sofa, your head on my lap, stroking your forehead, playing softly with your hair, soothing you . . . I just want to rest silently with and on you." In an investigation, the student testified that the professor had engaged in repeated unwanted kissing and touching and had several times insisted they share a bed.

When the investigation ruled in the student's favor and the university placed the professor on suspension for the 2018–19 academic year, a contingent of supporters came forward calling the charges a "malicious campaign." This superstar professor had a sterling reputation and would never do such things, they insisted. It all adds up to an all-too-familiar story, right down to the powerful colleagues who come forward to protect the aggressor.

The difference? The apparent predator here was a woman, Avital Ronell, and the victim, Nimrod Reitman, was a man.

WHAT THE DATA SHOWS

CTI data (see chapter 2) demonstrates that the central tenet of conventional wisdom holds true: the most common instance of workplace sexual misconduct is a senior man using his power to harass or assault a more junior woman. Women are more than two and a half times as likely to report harassment as men are, and 97 percent of these women say they were harassed by a man. Yet this all-too-common scenario *is not the only one*. More than one in eight women (13 percent) who report harassment say that the perpetrator was a woman. (These figures do not add up to 100 percent because a subgroup of women are harassed by both men and women.) Turning to assault, one in five women (20 percent) who report sexual assault say that the perpetrator was a woman (more on this in chapter 5, when I dig down into the high rates of sexual misconduct experienced by gay women). Even more startling, for men who experience sexual assault, it is twice as common for the perpetrator to be a woman than a man.

This data is deeply disturbing, and it flouts norms and expectations. It is also brand-new. No previous study has assembled a rich enough pool of data to allow identification of the perpetrator in terms of gender or race. The voices and the scholarship and the discussion presented in these chapters (3 through 5) should therefore be seen as a starting point in a research journey. I will take a stab at explaining what is going on, but these are early days and this book should not be seen as a definitive analysis of why some women prey on other women or why some Caucasians prey on people of color. And certainly, female misconduct can never justify male misconduct, or vice versa. But the data does affirm that women can be sexual predators, and men (particularly black men) can be sexual prey. These uncomfortable facts support the idea that the fundamental variable in workplace sexual misconduct is not "man" or "woman" but *power.*

WAITING TO SPEAK UP

Reitman finished his PhD at New York University under Ronell's supervision in 2015, but he waited two years to file his complaint. The reason, he says, was the same as that of the many actresses and witnesses who waited years or decades to speak up against Harvey Weinstein: it would have been career suicide.

Professors of literature and philosophy are not celebrities, but inside the academic world, Avital Ronell has enormous influence and authority—and her power over a young graduate student whom she supervises is near total. In some workplaces, there are objective performance metrics, such as sales or revenue. For graduate students in the humanities, professors' recommendations are the only currency that counts. The weight of objective measures, such as research papers published, largely depend on whether or not a well-known professor tells the world that this research is significant and rigorous.

Title IX of the Education Amendments of 1972 prohibits discrimination on the basis of sex in any federally funded education program or activity.[1] If a school knows or reasonably should know about sexual harassment or sexual violence that creates a hostile environment, it must take action. In May 2018, New York University found Professor Avital Ronell responsible for sexually harassing Nimrod Reitman, although the committee cleared her of allegations of sexual assault, stalking, and retaliation.

Reitman has since filed a lawsuit that alleges a recurrent pattern of sexual harassment, starting in May 2012. According to the lawsuit, that spring Ronell promised to introduce Reitman to prominent scholars in Paris and help him with his research. When he arrived in Paris, she insisted that he stay in her apartment and come into her bedroom to "read to her." Reitman says that though he "was mortified by this level of intimacy, he also did not want to anger or alienate his doctoral advisor, who was very insistent and had already shown a disturbing level of obsession with [him]." She subsequently insisted on staying in his New York apartment and sharing his bed for nearly a week. She also sent e-mails describing her desire for him.[2]

Curiously, both Reitman and Ronell identify as gay. Ronell has portrayed her messages as innocent expressions of affection "between two adults, a gay man and a queer woman, who share an Israeli heritage, as well as a penchant for florid and campy communications arising from our common academic backgrounds and sensibilities. These communications were repeatedly invited, responded to, and encouraged by him over a period of three years."[3]

We may never know exactly what transpired between Ronell and Reitman, but in her words it is hard not to hear echoes of a common "defense" that men dish up after abusing their power over a woman: *She was asking for it. She liked it. She never said no.* In short, aggressors often claim to have received consent. Perhaps they even believed that they did. But even presuming that Ronell is telling the truth, what does it mean when a junior person consents to or "encourages" a relationship with someone who holds complete power over his career? Ronell, a tenured professor in her sixties and a star in her field, could make or break Reitman, then in his twenties.

According to Reitman's lawsuit, "Ronell created a false romantic relationship between herself and Reitman and by threat of, among other things, not allowing him to advance his PhD, asserted complete domination and control over his life, both inside and outside of his academic endeavors. . . . He was required to be available to her all hours of the day and night, and to schedule his life around her wants and needs. Ronell forced Reitman to distance himself from friends and family, and she would often burst into a jealous rage when his attention was with them and not fully devoted to her."

In this lawsuit, Reitman also claimed that he considered transferring to a different advisor, but he feared that she would retaliate by giving him a poor recommendation that would scuttle his career, even though a subsequent advisor might be supportive. Much like the men who claim that retaliation against women who complain isn't retaliation, but justified dismissal for unrelated failures, Ronell responded to Reitman's lawsuit by claiming that Reitman, in whom she had invested years of her time, was not much of a talent after all. She said that "his main dilemma was the incoherency in his writing and lack of a recognizable argument."[4]

Like powerful men in similar predicaments, Ronell has had peers rally around her. "We deplore the damage that this legal proceeding causes [Ronell]," a group of scholars (many of them prominent feminists) wrote in an open letter, "and seek to register in clear terms our objection to any judgment against her." The letter cites her many academic accomplishments and awards, claiming, "There is arguably no more important figure in literary studies at New York University than Avital Ronell." It adds, "If she were to be terminated or relieved of her duties, the injustice would be widely recognized and opposed. The ensuing loss for the humanities, for New York University, and for intellectual life during these times would be no less than enormous and would rightly invite widespread and intense public scrutiny."[5]

Whatever may or may not have happened between Ronell and

Reitman, the letter follows a depressingly familiar playbook: a list of the powerful person's accomplishments, as if they were relevant to the discussion of possible guilt; and an emphasis on the threat to the institution where she works if she were to be in any way punished. None of Sebastian Tyler's pals, or the men supporting the "brilliant jerks" on Wall Street or in Silicon Valley, could have put it any better.

"If Avital Ronell struck a blow for feminism, it may lie in the fact that she believed she was so awesome that the rules about how to behave with other human beings didn't apply to her," the journalist Andrew O'Hehir wrote in *Salon*. "It's a widespread problem among my gender, but until very recently not among hers."[6]

NO ONE WAY TO BE A PERPETRATOR

The Italian actress Asia Argento was one of the first women to come forward with accusations against Harvey Weinstein. She said he had raped her and declared that his power over her career obliged her to submit to him for years. Once #MeToo broke the dam of silence, she became a vocal #MeToo advocate. However, soon after she took this public stance, it turned out that Argento may have committed an egregious act of sexual assault herself. A young man named Jimmy Bennett—who played her son in the movie *The Heart Is Deceitful above All Things*—accused her through his lawyer of plying him with liquor and forcing him to have sex with her in 2013, when she was thirty-seven and he was seventeen. Argento quietly agreed to pay Bennett $380,000.[7] Once Bennett's accusation and their deal became public, she alternately denied that anything sexual had taken place, declared that the payment was merely out of compassion and handled by her boyfriend,[8] and claimed that Bennett, "a boy with crazy hormones," had jumped on her.[9]

We may never know the details of what happened between Argento and Bennett, but the big picture appears clear. She was a powerful woman, more than twice his age, who had further authority over him from having known him since childhood. (In a creepy echo of those Catholic priests whom abused children called Father, Bennett often referred to her as his mother and she called him her son).[10] If, as she has admitted at times, they had a sexual relationship, it was both an abuse of power and statutory rape, since he was below the age of consent.

Tarana Burke, a founder of the #MeToo movement, summed up this point in a series of tweets: "I've said repeatedly," she wrote, "that the #metooMVMT is for all of us, including these brave young men who are now coming forward. It will continue to be jarring when we hear the names of some of our faves connected to sexual violence unless we shift from talking about individuals . . . and begin to talk about power. Sexual violence is about power and privilege. That doesn't change if the perpetrator is your favorite actress, activist, or professor of any gender."

In another tweet, Burke added: "A shift can happen. This movement is making space for possibility. But, it can only happen after we crack open the whole can of worms and get really comfortable with the uncomfortable reality that there is no one way to be a perpetrator."

SEX AND GETTING AHEAD

When I refer to women abusing their power in this chapter, I am not referring to a kind of sexual power that the sociologist

Catherine Hakim has named "erotic capital." Hakim makes a feminist argument that attractive young women should feel free to profit from "a complex but crucial combination of beauty, sex appeal, and skills of self-presentation."[11] In other words, Hakim suggests that young women should feel comfortable seeing their erotic power as a tool in their professional arsenal.

Certainly, plenty of women have taken that route. Some have used this "erotic capital" to complement remarkable professional abilities. Tina Brown is a case in point. In her twenties, she had an affair with Harold Evans, the editor of the newspaper where she worked (the *Times of London*). Evans was twenty-five years her senior and a powerhouse in the media world. He was also married, though several years later he divorced his first wife to marry Brown. Since that time, Brown has risen to great heights, becoming editor in chief of *Vanity Fair* and the *Daily Beast*, among other accomplishments. No one would deny Brown's formidable talents, and most of her success is surely due to those talents or her hard work. (Her marriage to Evans has also lasted to this day.) Still, marrying the editor of one of the UK's leading newspapers likely gave her a leg up at the start. Sir Harold undoubtedly opened doors for her.

Hakim believes that it's a mistake for feminists to ignore or downplay this form of power—instead she writes, women should acknowledge the reality of erotic capital and use it. Yet she does see danger lurking. She concedes that "men across the world treat women's erotic capital as a male right to possess" and that it fades over time.[12] Men almost exclusively like to hijack young women's erotic capital, which is why it's deeply problematic for a woman to rely on this asset: it doesn't perform in the long run. Suburbia and tony urban neighborhoods are littered with ex-wives who find themselves discarded for younger models.

As the CTI data presented in chapter 2 shows, even consensual relationships poison the work environment, causing big hits to dedication and commitment, respect for the parties involved, team performance, and team productivity. But even if those who try to flirt, sleep, or marry their way to the top are often foolhardy and they typically damage the workplace environment, they are not predators.

SEX AS AN INSTRUMENT OF POWER

The advantage men have had for so long is that they've held most of the stakes in the types of capital that last—and in fact tend to increase as the bearer grows older and more powerful. But women are starting to possess this more influential kind of capital. Avital Ronell is a case in point: she definitely *had* it; whether she revives her illustrious career remains to be seen.

What happens inside the head of someone who rises up the organizational totem pole? It could be that authority in the workplace, rather than gender per se, is what leads to sexual misconduct. According to a scholarly study of power and sex in the workplace, "sexual overperception" occurs when the newly powerful believe that they are now more sexually attractive to their subordinates—and they become more likely to view those subordinates as objects.[13] Naturally, there are plenty of respectful and considerate bosses, both men and women, who view their subordinates as valued professionals and even protégés. But there is a reason why CTI data found that 72 percent of women and 59 percent of men who reported harassment said that the perpetrator was someone senior to them.

It is certainly true that more men than women are workplace sexual predators; it is also true that more men than women have power—despite the progress of recent years, top jobs still elude women. When, in a TV interview, Bill Clinton was asked why he had had an affair with Monica Lewinsky, his answer was, at least, honest: "Because I could."[14] The concept of sexual overperception suggests that "it is plausible that once individuals are given power, motivated psychological processes will be observed to an equivalent degree in men and women."[15] In other words, as more women gain power over subordinates, they may act more like men and abuse that power more often.

FINGERS UP HIS BUTT

After Steven Ulmer[*] earned a master's degree in mental health counseling, he took a job in a university's psychology department. It would have been a good job, except for his boss. "She would put her hand in my pants and stick her fingers up my butt," Steven says. He complained to his supervisor. To that supervisor's credit, he actually took action and spoke to this woman's supervisors. She subsequently stopped groping Steven, but, he says, "She'd come up to me and say very sexual things. She wouldn't touch me, but I'd be at my desk and she'd come hovering really close. I'd tell her to back off, give me some space, and she wouldn't."

The strangest and most hurtful part, he says, was that his assailant had been a friend when they were in college together. Now he was a rung below her in the department hierarchy and, as best as he could tell, she seemed to have grown drunk with power.

"How can someone override that empathic side we're all supposed to have, especially with a friend?" he asks, before offering a possible answer to his own question. "Once a power differential

---

* Name changed at interviewee's request.

is established it gives a person, in their mind, the go-ahead to do whatever they want without any consequence," he says. "We were both in relationships. I just figured it had to be some kind of power thing, though it's hard to figure out where her mind was."

In early 2018, after only eight months on this job, which (aside from his boss) he liked a great deal, Steven asked the head of HR what would happen if he filed a complaint. The answer was a definitive *not very much*. "His view seemed to be that women get harassed, not the other way around," he says. Steven resigned and filed a complaint with the EEOC, which is still under investigation.

On the Silver Screen

It's been more than a quarter century since the novel (by Michael Crichton) and the movie (starring Demi Moore and Michael Douglas) came out, but the theme of *Disclosure* feels contemporary: an ambitious woman beats out an ex-boyfriend for a promotion, forces herself on him, then—when he spurns her—sets out to ruin his career. A critic at the time noted that the female protagonist "is not mentally unbalanced. Far from it. She is cool, in control—and utterly amoral."[16] It was a box office hit, taking in more than $214 million worldwide. Another Hollywood movie with a take on a woman harassing men—2011's *Horrible Bosses*— was a comedy. In one of that movie's subplots, Jennifer Aniston plays a dentist who harasses her male hygienist. It earned $209 million. However, the success of these films may, ironically, be a sign that society considers this scenario light entertainment rather than a grim problem. Movies that confront the far more common problem—men harassing women—have generally been viewed as depressing and have had nothing near the same profitability.[17]

WOMAN ON WOMAN

So far, I've talked about cases in which a man is the prey of a predatory woman. While men are the most frequent objects of female sexual misconduct, recall that the CTI survey found that women were the perpetrators in 13 percent of the harassment and 19 percent of the assault cases in which a woman was both the predator and the prey. A hip and outspoken New York entrepreneur named Miki Agrawal once gave voice to the phenomenon of female-on-female sexual aggression.

"I just love this taboo space," Agrawal told *New York* magazine. She is cofounder of Thinx, a company she helped kick off in 2011 that makes absorbent underwear and biodegradable tampons. It was branded as a sassy company, all about women flaunting their bodies and breaking taboos, with Agrawal positioning herself as an inspirational "modern day, badass female CEO."[18] She even started a foundation to teach girls around the world about menstruation and to help them respect and defend their own bodies.

But it seems that she broke a few "taboos" that exist to *protect* women: in 2017 her former public relations director, Chelsea Leibow, filed a complaint with New York City's Commission on Human Rights. Leibow alleged that Agrawal had publicly discussed the size and shape of female employees' breasts, in some cases touching and asking women to expose their breasts. Agrawal also shared nude photos of herself and asked employees to have sex with her. "I felt that Miki objectified my body when she declared that she was 'obsessed' with it and made very detailed comments about my breasts," Leibow said, "and it also seemed like a way for Miki to assert her dominance over female employees by simply doing whatever she wanted to do without asking, and showing she could get away with it." Soon after Leibow complained about this behavior, she was fired. According to Leibow, Agrawal cited a "disconnect in energy" as the main reason for her dismissal.[19]

Leibow is far from alone in facing workplace harassment from another woman. According to CTI data (see chapter 2), more than one in eight women who report harassment say that another woman was the perpetrator, and nearly one in five of those who suffered assault say that another woman was the assailant.

Thinx's board subsequently investigated Leibow's complaint and other, similar incidents. Agrawal was ousted as CEO, but—like so many men facing repeated and credible charges of misconduct— she seems to have bounced right back, getting funding for a new start-up named Tushy and finding a publisher for a new book, *Disrupt-Her.*

FEMINISM AND PREDATORY WOMEN

CTI data isn't the only evidence that women can be sexual predators in the workplace. Lara Stemple, a prominent legal scholar and an assistant dean and director of the Health and Human Rights Law Project at UCLA Law School has been studying sexual victim- ization at the hands of women for years. A study by Stemple and Ilan H. Meyer, also a professor at UCLA law school, published in the *American Journal of Public Health* in 2014, found even higher numbers than those found by CTI, based on data from four dif- ferent research centers. The National Crime Victimization Survey, for example, found that 38 percent of sexual violence was visited on men.[20]

A woman who rises within a very hierarchical organization— say, officer ranks in the military—is going to be able to wield power in many encounters. Stemple hasn't been surprised, therefore, to find that there are complaints of women harassing or abusing both men and women in the US military forces, though women made up only 3 percent of all assailants—or 146 reported cases—in 2017, according to the Department of Defense 2018 Annual Report on Sexual Assault in the Military. "The common one-dimensional portrayal of women as harmless victims reinforces outdated gender stereotypes," Stemple and Meyer wrote in a follow-up article in *Scientific American*. "This keeps us from seeing women as complex human beings, able to wield power, even in misguided or violent ways."

And the assumption that men are always perpetrators and never victims reinforces unhealthy ideas about men and their supposed invincibility. These hypermasculine ideals can reinforce aggressive male attitudes and, at the same time, callously stereotype male victims of sexual abuse as "failed men."[21] The *Atlantic* ran a story about the study called "When Men Are Raped." The magazine invited male readers to write in if they had been sexually assaulted by women. Harrowing stories appeared, including men who were drugged and raped or molested as children.[22]

Why, one might ask, would a feminist like Stemple—whose first job after law school was at the Center for Reproductive Rights, working on women's health issues, and whose second was with the Pacifica Institute for Women's Health—spend so much time studying abuse of men by women? The answer, she says, is that any movement that aims at fighting sexual abuse must take a more inclusive view: one that understands that the primary variable is not gender but power.

"I believe you can't stop sexual aggression without understanding how deeply ingrained it is as an abuse of power," she told me in an interview. "Feminist analysis has taught us that sexual victimization happens when there's an imbalance of power. Often that imbalance comes about when one person is male and one is female. But power manifests itself in a lot of other ways. Employers and employees, corrections officers and inmates, teachers and students; those are also relationships that exist with an imbalance of power."

A lot of the rhetoric around women as victims can be retrograde, Stemple says. "It can feel like it's reinforcing the outdated stereotypes that feminists ought to want to upend. The idea that women are voiceless, powerless, weak, naive, and virginal—and that men are the only ones who are interested in sex and aggressive power seeking. I think there should be one strand of feminism that allows us to make the case that we have to understand women in all the forms in which they come as humans. And sometimes they embody negative characteristics. To insist that women are these one-dimensional caricatures of vulnerability is, in my view, rather anti-feminist."

The psychologist Holly Richmond, a specialist in sexual assault, notes that in the view of society, "Women can be sexy, but when it comes to female pleasure for its own sake (not her partner's) and for her own sexual self-efficacy, we tend to take that much less seriously. To give a female sexual predator that much sexual power is culturally antithetical to what we've been taught."[23]

In some ways, the very existence of this problem is due to a feminist success story. Although progress has been disappointing, there have been real gains in female progression (more on this later). These days, at least some women are rising to the top of the ladder. This situation—women as top dogs in organizations—is so recent that key questions remain. For example, how precisely does power intersect with sexual desire for anyone who has enormous authority and control? And how does this intersection differ for men and women?

The fact that women lack an institutionalized foundation for sexual misconduct might help explain why a female predator often comes across as an outlier, a misfit, and why it might sound even crazier for Miki Agrawal to pass around nude photos of herself than for Charlie Rose to have female employees come to his house and walk around naked in front of him. No one excuses a woman's bad behavior by shrugging it off and saying "girls will be girls."

We are only beginning to tangle with these issues, but as we shall see, a focus on power relations in the workplace can explain a great deal of sexual misconduct—including some surprising data on men as victims, on people of color, and on the LGBTQ community. It can also point the way to solutions.

4

MEN AS PREY

Carl Murphy* had just started his job as a planning producer—"A pretty low form of life," he says—at a major television network, when he was asked to travel with the network's "million-dollar babe"—a star anchorwoman who had done wonders to the ratings. Carl's boss felt that the excursion—a short reporting trip to Memphis—would be a good experience for him. He gave Carl two commands: stay at the designated hotel, where the company had a good rate, and turn himself inside out supporting the star anchorwoman, because the network needed her happy. "People lost their jobs if they disagreed with her. If she felt they were not adequate, they were gone," Carl recalls. "She had that kind of power."

But the anchorwoman took one look at the hotel and refused to stay in it. Carl explained that they *had* to stay there. She walked across the street and booked rooms for them in another hotel. The rest of that day, at least, went smoothly. The anchor did the interviews that Carl had set up. He and the other producers created a script, which she was set to "track" (read aloud in a run-through) the next morning. The plan was then to return to New York. But in the morning, the anchor didn't show for her "track." Carl tried to call her, but he couldn't get through. So he went to her room

---

* Name has been changed.

and knocked. He could hear her on the phone, wrapping up a call. Carl waited. Finally, she came to the door—in a skimpy silk negligee.

She hadn't slept well, she said. She felt terrible and couldn't possibly read the script. And with that, she slipped back into bed. Nervous, standing by the door, Carl suggested that he could read the script to her. "I need a back rub," she said.

Caught between what he knew was the inappropriateness of her request and his fear of displeasing her, Carl sat in the chair next to her bed. She rolled over and threw the covers off, shrugging her shoulders as a gesture to him to start. Still sitting in his chair, Carl awkwardly stretched out his arms and massaged her back. "Who taught you to give a back rub?" she murmured. "That's terrible. Get on top of me and use both your hands."

"I am in a tie and shoes," he recalls. "I don't know what to do. So I get on the bed, I straddle her." From afar, it might sound like a male fantasy: a superattractive TV personality, in lingerie, inviting you, a much younger man, into her bed. But she wasn't just any knock-your-socks-off woman. She was Carl's boss's boss, the face of the company and someone his boss had ordered him to please. Adding to the pressure, Carl was a new hire in a dream television job and knew he was easily expendable.

As Carl recalls it, "I thought, *Am I supposed to sleep with her? If I do, this is the end of my career.* It is the least sexual thing that I have experienced in a long time—all I feel is fear, and childhood memories are flashing, too, of *Playboy* under the mattress. All of these images and questions and fears were happening at once." And then he felt her move her hips slightly, suggestively beneath him. "I think: *I am a dead man.*" But then the phone rang. Carl leaped up and answered it. It was his boss, asking for the anchor.

Carl gave her the phone, and when she got off, she was all business. She did the read-through and they went back to New York, where they recorded the show as scheduled. Neither mentioned this incident to each other again.

Over the years, Carl told the story to a few friends, always making it sound like a racy adventure. But today he sees it differently. He certainly recognizes that it could have been much, much worse—his career, for example, did not suffer—but he now sees that the anchorwoman had been abusing her power over him. "What if she had said, *Take off your clothes?*" he wonders. "What would I have done? I probably would have taken off my clothes. And I realized this must be what it feels like for so many women— this dance this powerful person put me through—before the whole thing goes off the rails."

WHAT THE NUMBERS TELL US

Thirteen percent of men have been sexually harassed at the workplace, CTI data shows. That's a bit more than a third of the level for women (34 percent), but it still means that one out of eight men have received unwanted and often humiliating sexual advances at work. Five percent of men have been sexually assaulted—only slightly below the seven percent of women surveyed who reported sexual assault.

When men are harassed and assaulted, the data (see chapter 2) show that the perpetrator is usually a woman. Sixty-eight percent of men who suffered harassment say that a woman was the perpetrator, as do 76 percent of men who suffered assault. But men harass and assault other men, too: 57 percent of male harassment victims cite a male perpetrator, and 38 percent of male assault victims say the assailant was a man. (Numbers add up to more than 100 percent, as a minority of men reported being abused by both women and men.)

As we shall see, when men suffer unwanted sexual advances and sexual contact, the pain and the shame go deep and are often hidden.

A MAESTRO—AND THE YOUNG MEN HE RULED

The music world saw James Levine as a genius, the greatest American conductor since Leonard Bernstein. As musical director of one of the world's most prestigious opera house—the New York Metropolitan—he made $27,000 each time he took the stage, on top of a $400,000 annual base salary. It was a rate, one music journalist said, "out of all proportion to anything else in the opera economy."[1] He held guest conductorships in the United States and Europe. He even arranged and conducted the soundtrack for a Walt Disney movie, *Fantasia 2000*. Meanwhile, for decades he had been using his power over young musicians to exploit them sexually.

In 1968 Levine told a twenty-year-old student of his, Albin Ifsich, "If we're going to work on your violin, I have to understand you sexually." He then proceeded to masturbate in front of him.[2] In the years that followed, Levine regularly fondled the young man, calling it an integral part of the young man's musical education. "I thought it was sex for my improvement, sex to make things better," Ifsich said. "Obviously that's not what it was, but I was led to believe that."[3]

"That was his selling point, that [the abuse] would help our musical development," said another former student, James Lestock, explaining why he drew closer to Levine. "And I desperately wanted to be a musician." Levine fondled Lestock in a hotel room. "When he asked me whether I wanted to have sex, my answer included the word 'no,'" Lestock said. "I tell people that I make sure to put quote marks around the word 'no' to make sure they know I spoke the word. But he continued on."[4]

Another young musician, Ashok Pai, filed a police report accusing the maestro of sexually abusing him as a teenager in the 1980s.[5] Ifsich and several other former "acolytes" of Levine described nightly gatherings at his house, which included ritual humiliation, sex with Levine, and mutual masturbation sessions.[6] Yet another man said that when he was seventeen years old, Levine gave him a prime spot in a student orchestra, lavished him with coaching and attention, then visited him at night and molested him. When the boy refused to let Levine repeat his abuse, the conductor ceased his coaching and attention.[7]

This appalling pattern sounds familiar: a famous person wields his power—stemming from celebrity, career clout, and financial leverage—to exploit his followers' bodies. The pattern includes complicity and cover-up as the famous person's peers rally around to protect the star who plays an outside role in feathering their collective nest. The Metropolitan Opera followed this script. As early as 1979 the Met's executive director received a letter describing Levine's sexual misconduct. He dismissed it as "scurrilous rumors [that] have been circulating for some months."[8] Yet Levine's behavior was, as it had to be, an open secret: a prominent older man cannot have nightly meetings with pretty young boys, for decades, without anyone suspecting a thing.

"Everybody in the classical music business at least since the 1980s has talked about Levine as a sex abuser," said Greg Sandow, a faculty member at Juilliard and former music critic for the *Village Voice*.[9]

Yet it was only in 2017 that some of Levine's victims came forward publicly, and only in March 2018, a year after the first credible, non-anonymous denunciations arrived at the Met, did the opera sever its ties with him. Levine (who has denied all accusations) was apparently able to prey on young men for at least fifty years. He could get away with it, in part, for the same reason that Harvey Weinstein and many other prominent men got away with abusing so many women for so long: they were so powerful they were deemed untouchable. But there is one big difference here: Levine's abuse was directed at men. When men are the prey the damage is different, and, on average, it appears even harder for them to speak up than it is for women.

STIGMA AND SILENCE

Very few men who have suffered sexual harassment or assault come forward to report it in official channels. Few even tell their friends. They didn't before #MeToo and they don't now. For many victims, such abuse cuts to the core of their masculine identity, violating what they think it means to be a man.

Women, too, often have kept silent about sexual misconduct, for some of the same reasons that discouraged me from reporting Sebastian Tyler's sexual abuse: most of my colleagues thought I had been "asking for it," and my only ally in the circle of power (Professor Coe) advised me not to lodge a formal complaint, since none of the top dogs would take action against the firm's top producer. But for a young woman to be the object of unwelcome male sexual attention is not (unfortunately) considered out of the ordinary; and for her to talk to a senior ally and ask for advice—and protection—is, for better or worse, rather traditional.

For most men, on the other hand, to be in either situation goes against the very definition of manhood. For centuries males have been taught that they need to be dominant and aggressive. "Men learn they're supposed to be in charge of sex. You're not supposed to be a victim, and if you are, then you're weak, you're not a real man," Howard Fradkin, a psychologist who has worked extensively with male survivors of sexual abuse and advised the US military on sexual assault, told me in an interview.

If another man is the harasser or assailer, a male victim may think himself unmanned: he was supposed to be tough and fight back. As he considers filing a complaint, he will worry about what other men would think of him if they knew that another man groped or raped him. He may also wonder how women will think of him and how his boss will look at him.

Such feelings are likely why, in the US armed forces, only 8 percent of men who suffer sexual assault ever file an official report about it. Women victims of assault in the armed forces also rarely report it, but their rate of reporting (22 percent) is still two and a half times greater.[10]

"To have another man abuse his power and take advantage of you can feel like one of the most emasculating and stigmatizing experiences a young man can have," writes Parker Hurley, a male model, when describing doing a photo shoot with the famous, enormously powerful fashion photographer Bruce Weber. Hurley was twenty-three at the time and said that those around him referred to Weber—then in his sixties—as a "god." At the photo shoot, this god orchestrated a bizarre bit of hand play to "feel the energy," which allowed him to grab Hurley's crotch. Hurley pushed Weber's hand away; Weber kept insisting; but Hurley was stronger. Weber finally removed his hand, muttered something about Hurley's lack of potential, then ended the photo shoot and sent him away. Hurley would never again have a chance to work for this god.[11]

Compared to Levine's victims, Hurley was lucky: he "merely" suffered a humiliating moment and lost a big career opportunity. Yet like most men in such situations, he did not speak up at the time—and, when he did, at first he only spoke anonymously. "I was scared," he wrote. He was not only scared of the damage that a "god" like Weber could do to his career. He was also scared of what the incident might do to other people's view of his manhood. "I was a victim of the pressure around what it means to be a man in today's society," he says.[12]

It is challenging for a young man to reject a towering authority figure, no matter how strong or how many muscles he has. Another model, Jason Boyce, tall and built like a Viking, described being in a daze when Weber groped him. Other men, he says, subsequently asked him why he didn't fight back, even beat up this dirty old man. But in the moment, the power of hierarchy and fame can easily overshadow the power of muscles. "When someone has a mental hold on you, anything physical goes out the window," Boyce said. "It doesn't matter how big or strong or awesome or fight-skilled you are."[13] (Weber has denied the accusations from Hurley, Boyce, and several other male models.)

If a man is harassed or assaulted by a woman, the pain and shame is even more complicated, because it is interlaced with ridicule. A man in such a situation may reasonably expect other men to make fun of him if he complains—there is, after all, a reason why Carl Murphy for years told the story of the anchorwoman not as the terrifying threat to his career that it was, but as a mouth-watering opportunity that was snatched away from him. A "real man," after all, is supposed to be thrilled if a "million-dollar babe" finds him sexy and comes on to him—it's the stuff of wet dreams. A man who *complains* about being forced into such a situation, even if it's with his boss's boss, who inspires terror rather than desire, might well fear that everyone—his colleagues, his boss, HR—would respond with laughter. Maybe he's a wimp, they might say. Maybe (with homophobia still so depressingly common) he's just gay, they'll say. He's certainly not one of the boys.

FURTHER ROADBLOCKS

Another reason for the silence of male victims isn't psychological, it's practical. If the law has done a poor job protecting women, it's done an even worse job protecting men. Consider how long it took Ohio State University to conduct an investigation into Dr. Richard H. Strauss. He was a sports physician at the school in the 1970s, '80s, and '90s. But it was not until May 2019 that an investigation concluded what many school officials had apparently known for decades and done little or nothing to stop; Dr. Strauss had groped or otherwise abused at least 177 male students over the course of his tenure. (He committed suicide in 2005.)

Until 2013, the FBI specifically defined rape as "the carnal knowledge of a female forcibly and against her will." The possibility of a man being raped simply didn't enter into it. This presumption, that a man can't be raped, "pervades even the most respected of institutions, including psychotherapy," writes attorney Siegmund Fred Fuchs.[14] Furthermore, Fuchs adds, a man may get an erection while being raped, as "a biological response that does not indicate consent or even sexual pleasure." Fuchs cites several examples, of men raped at gunpoint, or tied down, gagged, and blindfolded, yet still having erections, as well as male victims whose therapists question whether or not they really disliked being raped by a woman.

Yet most men assume that if they happened to have an erection, it's proof that they wanted it to happen. That belief can send a male victim into a vicious spiral of self-shaming. The sociologist Karen Weiss notes that "for more than thirty years, rape and sexual assault have been largely framed by activists as a women's safety issue and by feminist scholars as a substantive area within a broader violence against women literature."[15]

Until 1998, the law also assumed that a man could not suffer workplace sexual harassment—and therefore, if a sexual predator made a workplace intolerable for a man, he could not look to Title VII of the Civil Rights Act for recourse. It was the Supreme Court that finally plugged this gap in the law. The case involved Joseph Oncale, twenty-one years old in 1991 when he went to work on an oil rig off the Louisiana coast. Isolated offshore, Oncale had nowhere to run when coworkers and supervisors told him he had a "cute little ass," grabbed him in the shower, forced a bar of soap between his buttocks, and threatened to rape him anally. Oncale complained to his employer—who essentially said that to attract such attention, Oncale had to be gay. (He isn't.) Oncale resigned and filed a lawsuit, stating, "I felt that if I did not get away from my job, that I'd be raped." In 1998, the Supreme Court ruled (in a unanimous decision, written by Antonin Scalia, with a concurring opinion by Clarence Thomas) that Oncale had suffered sexual harassment that was discrimination, based on Title VII of the Civil Rights Act.[16]

As a justice, Scalia was not generally a strong supporter of employee and civil rights, but his opinion in this case is insightful: "Harassing conduct need not be motivated by sexual desire to support an inference of discrimination on the basis of sex," Scalia wrote, proceeding to give the example of a "harasser [who] is motivated by general hostility to the presence of women in the workplace."[17] Scalia is here touching on a fundamental truth: sexual harassment (or assault) may or may not be about desire, but it is always about power.

But even if workplace sexual misconduct for either gender is primarily about power, men and women express that power in different ways.

MEN ON MEN

What is the most manly institution in the United States? One can argue about the answer, but it seems that most people would put the military near or at the top of their list. It is also a highly hierarchical institution, with formal ranks that make clear who has power over whom. It has a long tradition of hazing rituals, to make power relations even more explicit. Finally, it is an institution somewhat separated from the rest of American life. This combination of a cult of manliness, explicit power relations, a history of hazing, and isolation make the military an ideal environment for sexual harassment and assault to take place—and for it to go unreported and unpunished.

The RAND Corporation found in 2014 that approximately 20,000 of the US military's 1.3 million active-duty members had experienced one or more sexual assaults in the twelve months just prior to its survey.[18] Howard Fradkin, who worked with RAND on this study, stresses that 60 percent of these 20,000 military victims are men. Also according to this study, "Penetrative assaults against men were more likely to involve injuries and threats of violence; men were more likely to describe the event as serving to humiliate or abuse them as opposed to having a sexual intent, and they were more likely than women to describe the assault as hazing (34 percent of men who were assaulted described the assault as hazing; 6 percent of women did so)."[19]

Perhaps the best-known incident is that of Heath Phillips, who joined the navy when he was just shy of seventeen years old. Right before he shipped out on his first assignment, a group of shipmates drugged and gang-raped him. Aboard ship, they continued their abuse, forcing his mouth open, shoving their genitals in, and telling Phillips that if he bit, they would kill him.

Like 92 percent of his fellow victims of assault in the armed forces, Phillips did not file a formal complaint. As a teenage enlisted man, the lowest of the low, the thought did not even occur to him. He quit the navy, then lost the next twenty years of his life to substance abuse and depression. One icy night in February 2009, driving his truck through a vodka-and-pill-induced haze, he looked for a tree to crash into. He never found the right tree; instead he remembers waking up in his truck and being hit with the revelation: "I need help." From that day, which he describes as the moment he hit rock bottom, he went into therapy and began to grapple with what had happened to him. After therapy, he went public with his story and became an activist for reform in how sexual misconduct in the military is investigated, reported, and punished. In his new life, he has heard from hundreds of military men and women who have suffered assaults.

"To me sexual assault isn't a gender issue," Phillips told me in an interview. "It's all about power." As he sees it now, gang-raping a new recruit was hazing, a way for stronger and slightly more senior sailors—whom, he subsequently learned, had similarly attacked seventeen other young men aboard the same ship—to establish dominance. "What they were doing was pretty standard but [at the time] nobody cared," says Phillips. "When I tried to tell my commanding officer, he called me a liar and said, 'You must be homesick.'"

Obviously, only a small minority of military men rape new recruits, but such incidents are a particularly stark demonstration of how sexual assault is used to establish dominance. The corporate world's rites of passage may be subtler than those for men in the marines or navy, but the workplace is still a context where men deliberately create cultures of toxic masculinity that reinforce power structures and gender norms. They might do so by showing pornography at work, making jokes laden with crude sexual imagery, teasing other men about their anatomy, or encouraging a wink-wink, nudge-nudge approach to sexual harassment, with the unspoken message that this is what the alpha males in the room do to women—and maybe to other men if they're less macho—or to male bystanders who object to such behavior. A 2016 study, for example, found that men who engage in feminist activism are more likely themselves to become targets of sexual harassment because they're seen as having deviated from traditional masculine expectations.[20]

Cultures of toxic masculinity rest, in part, on fears of retaliation. Employees at the hedge fund giant Bridgewater, for example, described (in a National Labor Relations Board complaint) pressures to conform to a behavioral model of aggressive masculinity, including visits to a strip club.[21] In a complaint filed with the Connecticut Commission on Human Rights and Opportunities in 2016, a young male analyst named Christopher Tarui said that his supervisor had groped him, obliged him to watch videos of him having sex with another man, and repeatedly proposed that the two have sex. After Tarui refused, his supervisor dinged his performance rating. Tarui waited months to lodge a complaint, fearful that the incident would not remain private and would be used against him. When he did finally complain, he claims that top managers confronted him, urged him to withdraw his complaint, and accused him of "blowing this whole thing out of proportion."[22]

Tarui was brave enough to risk antagonizing his immediate supervisor and his supervisor's supervisors, while putting in jeopardy his career at perhaps the world's preeminent hedge fund. But for every man like Tarui who speaks up—risking retaliation and worse—many others keep quiet. In the armed forces, for example, the RAND Corporation found that only one third of men who suffered sexual harassment reported it. (By comparison, 46 percent of women who suffered harassment in the armed forces reported it.)[23] The result of such silence is that men in power, with the help of other men in power, can force their subordinates to submit.

GETTING FIRED FOR WALKING AWAY

When Evan Grover[*] was in his early thirties, he was a product manager at a bank. His boss was a woman about ten years older. "Her actions were a little bit more than flirtatious on the job," he recalls. "Maybe a hand on the leg. If a woman does that I don't necessarily think much about it, because as men we're not brought up to recognize those cues. I knew a woman would mind if I did that to her, but when this woman did it I just thought, okay I guess she likes me—not thinking, oooohh, she *likes* me."

The team frequently went out as a group after work. One Friday

* Name changed at interviewee's request.

night, his boss had way too much to drink. "I saw that she was inebriated, and I thought she needed some help getting home, so I got in a cab with her and made sure she got to her apartment," says Evan. "She kept insisting that I come in for another drink, and when I tried to close the door and leave she stuck her foot in the way. My reaction was *Is what I'm thinking really what's happening?* For a moment it was even kind of an ego boost, but I quickly began to feel uncomfortable. When you want to leave, and she keeps pushing, and she's your boss, it becomes less about flattery and more about *How do I get out of this situation without losing my job?*"

He finally walked away. When he went into the office on Monday she acted as if nothing had happened. She neither asked about his weekend, as she usually did, nor thanked him for seeing her home. He left the office briefly, and when he came back and sat down at his computer, he had a nasty surprise. His account was frozen. His boss had fired him.

When your boss fires you in this way, your problems are just beginning. You can't use her as a reference. And, if you're a man, you're probably afraid to tell the truth about why you were fired. So Evan did the only possible thing: he changed fields. "I got out of banking for a couple of years, so that I'd have enough of a break that not having her as a reference wasn't as important," he says. He later learned from former colleagues at the bank that his boss's advances to him had been part of a pattern. "The profile was men who were younger and a bit shy," he says. "Junior, inexperienced people who wouldn't speak up, who wouldn't go to HR. I wasn't her first target."

Evan's professional life has turned out just fine, even if he had to abandon the career he had long worked for and planned on. He has started his own business and even does work now and then for banks on a contract basis. But his personal life, he believes, has suffered. "I think about how passive I was and didn't do anything, like go to HR. If I had done something about her harassment, it might have had a different impact on my other relationships," says Evan, who recently went through an acrimonious divorce.

Given societal expectations, feelings of powerlessness in the wake of sexual harassment and assault seem to be particularly damaging to men. Even more so than women, they engage in self-blame and elect to remain silent. These additional layers of shame help explain why CTI data shows that men's job satisfaction falls to 39 percent from 56 percent when they suffer harassment at work, while women's job satisfaction falls less precipitously (from 56 percent to 48 percent).

For some men, especially when the misconduct they suffer is sexual assault, self-blame hardens into self-hate, which in turn often triggers severe depression and substance abuse, as it did for Phillips. And for nearly all men who suffer harassment or assault, whether they are a gifted teenage boy whom a maestro draws under his spell or a highly successful man in his thirties earning a large salary at a hedge fund being hit upon by a supervisor, fear of being mocked or ridiculed by others encourages silence.

As we will see in chapter 5, it is not just men whose experience of sexual harassment and assault differs from the cases highlighted by the #MeToo movement. Both people of color and LGBTQ employees face special burdens, which the media narrative surrounding #MeToo has often ignored.

Creepy Flirting

Phil La Duke, based in the Detroit area, is a consultant specializing in workplace safety and organizational change—and he has taught classes in sexual harassment avoidance. "When a woman starts telling a man he's hot or sexy at work," he notes, "everyone thinks she's just being flirty, but if it isn't invited, it's creepy." La Duke knows about creepy flirting. He experienced it himself, twice. The first time, he was nineteen and working behind the counter of a fast-food franchise to pay his way through college. The franchise manager, a divorced woman in her forties, had a few discomforting habits.

"Once," he says, "she asked me if I thought a customer who was wearing a push-up bra that made her nipples clearly visible was sexy. I didn't answer and I walked away. Then she started calling me into meetings in the office behind the kitchen, where she did things like put her hands on my butt and rub her breasts against me. Then she hired her daughter and started pressuring me to ask her daughter out. I felt it was an extremely bad idea for me to date a coworker who was also the boss's daughter."

In response to his lack of response, the manager cut his workweek from forty hours to two: an hour at lunchtime on Mondays and another hour on Fridays. But La Duke had read up on employment laws and knew how to defend himself. "I told her that if she didn't restore my hours and knock off the harassment, I would make three phone calls: one to my lawyer, one to the head of HR, and one to the newspaper. That shook her up and she restored my hours and left me alone."

The second incident occurred fifteen years later, when he was developing content for a training and consulting firm. The administrative assistant to the firm's owner began to hit on him. "Once, she put her hand on my shoulder, so I reached over and moved it off. She asked if I'd go out to dinner with her that night. I said I had to go home and make dinner for my daughter. She said, 'I could come over.' I told her no. Then she put her hand on me again and I again removed it. Then she said, 'You know, you could get into real trouble if I told anyone you were touching me.'" Fortunately for La Duke, soon after this interaction the firm fired the woman for incompetence.

5

CROSSING LINES OF RACE AND SEXUAL ORIENTATION

Terry Crews, a star of the television show *Brooklyn Nine-Nine*, is six foot three, 245 pounds, and—a former NFL linebacker—full of muscles. He is married, with five children and a grandchild, and he speaks frequently about his Christian faith.[1] Surely, one would think, such a man would be the last one on earth to be sexually harassed and groped by another man—especially at an event where Crews's wife was present.

But in February 2016, when Crews and his wife were at a party together, a high-profile Hollywood agent, Adam Venit, looked at Crews from across the room and began making suggestive gestures with his tongue. Crews at first assumed that Venit was making a joke. He was wrong. "He comes over to me. I stick my hand out, and he literally takes his hand and puts it on my genitals and squeezes. I jump back like, 'Hey, hey.' And he's still poking his tongue out and all this stuff, and I go, 'Dude, what are you doing? What are you doing?' and then he comes back at me again. He just won't stop."

Crews could have yelled. He also could have violently shoved this much smaller man away. But it was a work-related party, full of Hollywood power players whom Crews either worked for or might work for in the future. He'd never met Venit before, but Venit's agency represented Crews. There also was a shock factor. "When a person of power breaks a boundary and violates a boundary, you're a prisoner of war," Crews said.[2] Finally, there was another factor, the most important of all, one that inhibited Crews and may have disinhibited Venit: Venit is white and Crews is black.

Crews said that his first instinct was indeed to pummel this man who was groping him, but he quickly recognized that, as a black man, it was the worst thing he could do. When he testified before the United States Senate Committee on the Judiciary in 2018, in support of the Sexual Assault Survivors' Bill of Rights, a sympathetic senator, Dianne Feinstein, asked, "Why weren't you violent? You're a big, powerful man."

"Senator," Crews answered, his voice choking up, "as a black man in America, you only have a few chances to make yourself a viable member of the community . . . I'm from Flint, Michigan. I have seen many, many young black men who were provoked into violence, and they either ended up in prison or were killed . . ." He then described how his wife had spent years preparing him to keep cool if someone ever tested his limits. "She said if you ever get goaded, if you ever get prodded, if you ever have anyone try to push you into any kind of situation, don't do it, don't be violent," he told the Senate. "I'll be honest, it was the strength of my wife . . . the training worked, because I did not go into my first reaction. I grabbed her hand, we left [the party], but the next day I went right to the agency. I said this is unacceptable. I told them how I almost got violent but I didn't. I said what are you going to do about this predator that you have roaming your hallways?"

Venit subsequently called to apologize, but for Crews that was not enough. He wanted the agency to take some sort of action against this man. They didn't. "I was told they were going to do everything in their power . . . and then they disappeared." Yet

Crews did not go public at the time or try to pressure the agency further. What would a man, whose career is in part built on how stereotypically manly he appears, benefit from recounting how he let another man grope him? Would anyone even believe it?

Like so many others, men and women, who over the years have "shut up and put up," it took the #MeToo movement to enable Crews to speak up. "Once I saw some of Weinstein's victims came forward," he told the Senate, "it actually empowered me to tell my story."[3] Crews started his revelation by tweeting that "a high-level Hollywood executive" had assaulted him. He then named and shamed Venit on television, filed a complaint with the Los Angeles police, stopped letting the agency where Venit worked represent him, and filed a civil lawsuit against the agency. He settled the lawsuit once the agency agreed to his demands: Venit resigned and the agency instituted policies intended to prevent similar abuses.

As I see it, Crews is one of the bravest of those who have come forward and denounced a sexual predator. His case also illustrates an especially ugly aspect of American culture: many white men and women see black men (and black women) as fair game or safe targets for sexual abuse, and many black men—like Crews—face additional layers of pain, shame, and damage.

WHAT THE DATA SHOWS

Twenty-one percent of black men say they have been sexually harassed at work, compared to 13 percent of all other men. Seven percent of black men and 7 percent of Latino men say they have been sexually assaulted at work, compared to 4 percent of white men. In other words, black men are one and a half times more likely to experience harassment than other men, and black and

Latino men are nearly twice as likely to experience sexual assault as white men.

Women of all races experience the same level of sexual assault (all cohorts hover around 7 percent), but Latina women experience slightly above-average levels of harassment (37 percent, compared to the 34 percent average), while black and Asian women experience less (23 percent).

For LGBTQ employees, meanwhile, the numbers are off the charts: 9 percent of LGBTQ men experience assault and 23 percent experience harassment at work, according to CTI's survey—nearly double the levels for men as a whole. Meanwhile 10 percent of LGBTQ women report assault and 43 percent experience harassment at work: staggering numbers that are one and a half times the rates for women as a whole.

This new data offers a rare glimpse of the damage done by sexual abuse to a range of vulnerable groups in the white-collar workforce. The figures are enormously distressing, since they describe pockets of pain that have been largely buried—covered by stigma, suspicion, fear, and silence. But these figures also point forward. They illustrate why the #MeToo movement must become more inclusive, reaching beyond young white women to proactively embrace people of color as well as LGBTQ employees. They also demonstrate the degree to which sexual misconduct at work is fundamentally about power. For decades American society has demeaned and demonized whole categories of people and rendered them powerless. Sexual harassment and assault have been central to the onslaught, part of the arsenal and a weapon of choice.

I'll now dig into what this looks like for these communities, though I wish, as an outsider to these communities, to do so humbly. Although I'll do my best, I do not pretend that this chapter is a definitive depiction of the experience of people of color and LGBTQ communities. Instead, I hope to offer a starting point to understand these pain points, an outline for further research, and an invitation for more voices to come forward.

MEN OF COLOR

Soon after Terry Crews delivered his Senate testimony, the rapper 50 Cent (Curtis Jackson) gave his response via Twitter: his tweet featured a photo of a shirtless, muscle-bound Crews saying "I got raped. My wife just watched." Another tweet of his said: "LOL, what the ___ is going on out here man . . . THEY would have had to take me to jail." The hip-hop producer Russell Simmons—whom several women have accused of raping them—e-mailed Crews to say, "Give the agent a pass . . . ask that he be reinstated." In other words, these celebrities decided to *blame* Crews: either for not fighting back at the time or for speaking up and denouncing Venit later.

Black men face a long, ugly history of being falsely accused of sexual harassment and assault. That horrifying history likely explains why many black men and women are hesitant to rush to judgment against a man who is accused of sexual misconduct. As Crews points out, these historic injustices encourage black men to believe they have to be tough in ways that are deeply misogynist. Rap lyrics that routinely use such terms as "ho" and "bitch" to refer to women reflect these distortions. In a *Time* magazine interview in 2017, Crews looked back on his own place in what he called "the cult of masculinity," especially as practiced by African American men. "I've been to the rally for civil rights, and they will look at a woman and say, 'Bitch, sit down,'" Crews said. "And you're like, 'Wait a minute—this is civil rights here . . . How are you going to get justice, and you aren't even treating the women in your circle with justice?'"[4]

In related ways, many black men who suffer assault must also endure particularly brutal societal stereotypes. "People have said this sexual assault against strong black men can't be true," Jay Connor told me in an interview. Connor, a Los Angeles–based writer, wrote an article in the *Huffington Post*—"Strong Black Men Are Victims of Assault Too"—to defend Crews against those who criticized him for being assaulted and for speaking up. "Inherently," Connor told me, "we've got to be strong because we've got to deal with racism and all this other stuff. It makes it difficult culturally for us to be vulnerable. So when situations like this occur, black men don't feel comfortable with addressing how they feel about it or that it really happened. . . . It's like it's a sign of weakness. I can't let anybody know this happened; I ain't gay, I ain't no punk."

Black men face other dangers, too: they may be blamed for any misconduct, even when they are the victims. It's why Crews didn't dare fend off his assailant with physical force. It's why a black doctor told *Slate* that when workplace sexual banter gets too graphic, he walks off, for fear that, "when the supervisor or whoever asks, 'Who was there?' the response is, 'Three nurses and the black guy.'" It's why another black doctor who was targeted by a white female nurse who had grabbed his crotch and refused to take no for an answer knew that he couldn't complain to the hospital where they both worked.[5] Scholarly research has shown that black men tread on eggshells in their workplace interactions, especially with white women, to avoid evoking caricatures of oversexed and predatory black males.[6]

EMASCULATION, FETISHIZATION, AND THE ABUSE OF POWER

"As I shared my story I was told over and over that this was just a joke, that this was just horseplay," Crews told the Senate Judiciary Committee. "But I can say that one man's horseplay is another man's humiliation. . . . What Venit was effectively telling me while he held my genitals in his hand was that he held the power, that he was in control."

As I noted earlier, sexual harassment and assault can be a workplace weapon, designed to keep those outside the dominant group "in their place"—shut out of pivotal roles, promotions, and positions of power. Black men have often faced a particularly ugly variant of this weaponization: not only are black men often viewed as predators, but their bodies may become fetishes, objects on which white people feel entitled to indulge their desires.

"I know the fantasy exists. It renders black men desired on one hand and feared on the other," Wesley Morris, a gay African American man, wrote. "You can read the history of the black penis in this country as a matter of eminent domain: if a slave master owned you, he also owned your body."[7] Fetishization of black men has long been a commercial venture. To take just one example, a club called Arousals, in the small English town of Dunstable, sponsors a swingers' night "for white women who want to have sex with black men, and their white husbands or partners who want to watch." A journalist summed up the night as "humiliation-themed, racially based sexual fantasies."[8]

Unlike Terry Crews, Warren Thomas* is not a Hollywood star with a linebacker's physique. Recently retired after a long career as an executive in the retail sector, he is an older, dignified black

* Name changed at interviewee's request.

man of average build. He prides himself on his forty-year marriage, his successful children, and his deeply satisfying family
life. In the fall of 2018, I talked to him about new CTI data that
indicated that black men suffer above-average rates of sexual harassment and assault in the workplace. He offered to tell his story.

At his last job, a white female executive—both younger and more
junior than he was—regularly sidled up to him at company events
and told him, in a loud whisper that others could hear, that he was
a "black stud." When no one else could see, she plastered herself
against him and grabbed his butt. Like so many other black men
in such a situation, Thomas tried to avoid her but otherwise kept
quiet. What would happen if a black man accused a white woman
of groping and harassing him? At best, he might become an office
joke. At worst, the white woman might turn the tables and say that
he was assaulting her.

The moment of reckoning came when, at a team off-site, she
found out the number of his hotel room, showed up half naked,
and refused to leave. Thomas called hotel security, who escorted
her back to her room. The next day he went to the police, filed for
a restraining order—which was granted—and told the company's
CEO what had happened. From then on, Thomas was at least able
to work in peace, but the career consequences that this woman faced
were, precisely, zero. She kept rising up the ranks. The firm's CEO
apparently saw no objection to continuing to promote an employee
whom another employee had to seek police protection against.

LATINAS ARE ESPECIALLY TARGETED

"They all know I won't report. I'm too vulnerable. I'm a newcomer
fighting for a spot in the sun with a lot to lose." That was how Maria

Mendonça,[*] a manager on the digital design team at a PR firm in Washington, DC, explained her decision not to report an obvious, explicit case of sexual harassment. Maria, like many women of color, feels she is at the bottom of the totem pole—and in her case, her lowly status is exacerbated by the fact that she is also an immigrant, from Brazil.

The incident that she—still visibly shaken—told me about had occurred a few weeks earlier at her company's holiday party. "I was hanging out with my boss, Eric,[*] and two other executives on the team. We were having fun, laughing. I'd had a couple of glasses of wine and was feeling great. I finally felt that I belonged on the team, that these were my friends. Then, all of sudden, Eric yanked me to one side and propositioned me. He didn't bother with any niceties. 'You're hot,' he said, 'I want to ___ you. Come back to my hotel. I'm leaving now. Go get your coat.'"

"You're crazy," Maria said, pulling away. "You're married and so am I." She stuck her left hand out and tapped her wedding ring. He let out a laugh and said, "I'm thinking that doesn't mean much to you people." Grabbing her around the waist, he pushed her toward the coat check. "Come. I want you to show me your sexy Brazilian bikini wax."

Desperate to escape her boss, who had her by the waist, Maria, accidentally on purpose, spilled her glass of red wine down his shirt. He let go with a yelp of surprise and she ran to the ladies' room, where she waited until the party ended—two hours later. While she was hiding out there, a colleague, Kate, walked in. "I know her well," Maria says, "she sits in the cubicle next to me. 'Oh my God,' I told her, 'I can't believe what just happened, Eric just propositioned me, asked me to go back to his hotel room. I don't know what to do. Has something like this ever happened

* Name changed at interviewee's request.

to you?' Kate stopped in her tracks (she was fixing her hair), spun around, and snapped. 'Of course not, he wouldn't dare. *You* must have done something to egg him on.'"

Now, Maria says, she can't sleep at night, afraid that Eric will retaliate. "Just yesterday he was in the office and walked right past me. He turned and stared at me and his eyes radiated anger. I know he's going to fabricate some performance shortcoming and get rid of me. I'm just waiting for it to happen."

I asked Maria why she didn't just go to HR and lodge a complaint. I know her company—it has an impressive "zero tolerance" policy toward sexual harassment—and there were witnesses. Maria just stared at me for a moment, shocked at my naivety. "Look," she said. "I'm an immigrant. It was a long, hard struggle to land this job. I had credentials, experience, and a green card, but recruiters would see my name and nationality and strike me off the list. I'm not the right kind of immigrant. Qualified foreigners from the UK and Australia can get jobs easily. But if you're from Latin America or Africa? Forget it.

"Besides which, I'm a Brazilian woman. Everyone thinks we have loose morals and are 'hot to trot.' Just yesterday two colleagues were joking around about Carnival being around the corner. One asked me if I was stocking up on teeny bikinis and Trojans, the other asked me how many times I was planning to get laid. 'Isn't this the time of year you all make out with whomever you want?' he said. They both laughed uproariously." Maria then reminded me of her colleague Kate's reaction. "If that's the response of a female colleague, someone I thought of as a friend, what should I expect from HR?"

One Wall Street CDO told me that she was disappointed but "unsurprised" by Maria's experience. "In the media, whether that's television or even cable news, there's a narrative around how glamorous and sexy Latina women are," she told me. "Sometimes all you hear about, it seems, are the bikinis."

A professor at Columbia Law School, Kimberlé Crenshaw, coined a term that helps explain the experience of Maria and so many other woman of color when faced with sexual abuse: *intersectionality*.[9] Crenshaw originally applied this concept—discrimination due to multiple factors at once—to black women in particular, and several studies have since confirmed that racial and sexual harassment intersect in the workplace. One study, for example, of ninety-one African American women suing their employer over sexual harassment found that the women who had experienced the most frequent sexual harassment also reported more frequent racial harassment. The intersections that underlie discrimination may, of course, include far more than just these two factors. "Harassment can target a multitude of factors besides gender and race, such as social class, sexual orientation, or disability status," the study's authors wrote.[10]

What applies to black women also applies to Latinas and (as we shall see) members of the LGBTQ community. In addition, a woman who is Latina or black (or both) will likely face two overlapping burdens: her own culture's view of a woman's role and the broader American view of "outsider" women.

"Even if people don't know my nationality, they think Latinas occupy a specific space, of being hyper-sexed," says Zahira Kelly-Cabrera, an Afro-Dominican writer, artist, and critic. "I get a double dose of it being black."[11] Kelly-Cabrera's first job after college in the United States was at an NGO where most of the staff were Latino men. The men constantly harassed her, as did her boss. They tried to sleep with her and falsely boasted to each other that they had. Still, for a long time she didn't speak up. She was so used to men treating her that way that, she says, "I didn't have a concept of it being bad or illegal."

"Latina women in less-skilled occupations," writes the lawyer Waleska Suero, "are often immigrants who are either unfamiliar with US sexual harassment laws or feel that their jobs are too vulnerable to risk complaining."[12] Many, of course, are unfortunately correct about that, and it may apply to Latinas in more-skilled occupations, too, as Maria Mendonça's story illustrates.

Women of color face many types of risk when they speak up. Kelly-Cabrera, for example—who increasingly blogs, posts, and writes about sexual assaults on women of color—attracts two kinds of readers: fifty thousand online followers who are inspired by her words and hundreds of online harassers.

"I've had messages," she told me in an interview, "that say, 'You should get raped,' 'I hope you get raped,' and 'I'm going to rape you.' I've had as many as three thousand hate messages in my inbox at one time," she says. Such hate mail is a horrifying confirmation of the fact that sexual harassment and assault is about power. These men threatening Kelly-Cabrera with rape are evidently not expressing their attraction to her. They are expressing a wish to punish her for speaking out and they are aiming through their harassment to "put her in her place."

Generational Disconnect— or Just Plain Sexual Misconduct?

Despite the enormous strides made by the LGBTQ community on the human rights front, gay culture doesn't necessarily ensure a safe space. John Duran, who served as mayor of West

Hollywood in greater Los Angeles from 2018 to 2019, ran his administration as if it were his personal fiefdom in the town that is home to the legendary Sunset Strip and the trendiest gay nightlife in town. Duran once joked about wearing gold lamé underwear while speaking from the City Council dais.

But in 2016 his former council deputy accused him of sexual harassment. The city paid out $500,000 to settle. In 2019, with new allegations from three current or former members of the Gay Men's Chorus of Los Angeles, a number of residents and politicians called for Duran to step down. Chorus members described him slipping his hand inside their waistbands and making various inappropriate comments.

The men were all in their twenties, and Duran, who was fifty-nine, blamed #MeToo. "There's a culture clash going on," he told the *Los Angeles Times*. "If somebody expresses himself or herself sexually, that doesn't make it harassment, per se." His targets disagreed. One said he knew "lots of older gay men who definitely understand the idea of consent."

In early March, Duran announced that he would step down as mayor, implying that health problems were the reason, and promising he would "be back as feisty as ever very soon."[13]

LGBTQ EMPLOYEES

There is something, alas, so fundamental that it appears to unite all races and genders: a tendency to view LGBTQ employees as powerless and easily cowed that they can be harassed or assaulted with impunity. CTI data (see chapter 2) shows that LGBTQ men are more likely than heterosexual women to report assault, while LGBTQ women are the most commonly harassed group of all. Often intersectionality strikes here, too: when an LGBTQ individual is also a person of color, he/she may be even more targeted by predators.

Consider Kamran Hamid,[*] who a few years back was moving up the ranks in the IT department of a global pharmaceuticals company. On a Friday afternoon in the fall of 2016, he and his team went out for a few drinks after work to celebrate: they had just "sorted" a huge incompatibility problem within the company's newly acquired biotech division. Smelling big year-end bonuses, the team was ready to party. By 9 p.m., everyone was at least a little tipsy, and Roger Evans,[*] the SVP who had led this project—was plastered. He was sitting on top of the bar, shirt unbuttoned, fly partially unzipped, surrounded by empty shot glasses and raucous men. Sighting Kamran, Roger drunkenly waved him over.

Kamran pretended not to see and slipped outside for a smoke. Five minutes later Roger came charging out. "He just went straight for me," Kamran told me, "grabbing and twisting my necktie and pushing me up against the nearest wall. He then jammed his face in front of mine and started spewing poison. 'You think you're a poster boy, don't you? Well fuck all this diversity crap, all you are is a dirty brown faggot, and I'm thinking you need a little roughing up, to help you get things in perspective.' Roger let out a baying laugh, and twisted my necktie even harder. It became so tight that I started gagging and tearing up. Then, keeping a lock on my tie with one hand, he reached down with the other and started undoing my belt. By now a crowd had gathered, and as he fumbled with my buckle a woman gasped loudly. That somehow broke the

* Name changed at interviewee's request.

spell. People stopped just looking. Two big guys came forward and pulled Roger off me."

With that, Kamran was safe from physical harm—but, Roger had already succeeded in demonstrating who was top dog. "The depth of my humiliation," Kamran told me, "is hard to describe. People tried to help, offering me ice cubes and wet napkins for my neck, which had red score marks from where Roger had attempted to strangle me with my tie. But I couldn't deal with them; I ducked out of bar and fled the scene. I didn't want pity and I especially didn't want my colleagues to see me as this slobbering, shattered wreck. I walked the streets for hours until I was calm enough to drive home. One thing that obsessed me: one of the guys who pulled Roger off of me was a direct report of mine. How was I going to face him Monday morning?"

Over the weekend, other thoughts crowded in. As Kamran recounts it: "I kept on asking myself, what was the *real* trigger? What made Roger want to take me down so brutally? Was it because I'm a brown Middle Easterner, or because I'm gay? By Sunday night Kamran had given up on deep questions and had only one thing on his mind, how to get out of this situation without ruining his career. Monday morning he applied for a transfer to another part of the company.

Kamran gave no reason for his request. He did not denounce Roger to anyone or file a complaint with HR. As far as he was concerned, more than enough people already knew about his humiliation. He wasn't out for justice. He just wanted to get away, right away. So when the company agreed to organize a transfer, but said that the only role open would be a demotion, he accepted: this new position was in Munich, which meant that Kamran would be far away from Roger. Six months later he got even farther away, jumping ship to join a competitor. Roger stayed at his job. He was, after all, a big producer and no one else came forward to denounce him. Perhaps Roger passed it all off as "horseplay."

Would Roger have felt so free to publicly assault Kamran if Kamran hadn't openly identified as gay? Or if he had been white? It's impossible to know, but this much is clear: Roger harassed and assaulted Kamran because he believed that he could do so with impunity. When Roger called Kamran a "dirty brown faggot" outside a crowded bar in front of his whole team, he clearly wanted the world to know that he, not Kamran, held all the cards.

Unfortunately, Roger was right. It was Kamran, not Roger, who took a demotion and left. This incident took place three years ago, and one hopes that today, after #MeToo, a man like Kamran would speak up, go to the police, file a complaint, and demand justice. But I suspect that there are still plenty of Rogers out there, acting abusively, and plenty of Kamrans, keeping silent—in part because the legal system does a particularly poor job of protecting LGBTQ individuals in the workplace.

More than three decades after the US Supreme Court first ruled that sexual harassment is sex discrimination, the courts are still divided on whether Title VII, the 1964 law that bars such discrimination in the workplace, extends to sexual orientation. The US District Court for the Eastern District of New York, for example, ruled that Title VII does *not* provide protection for sexual orientation. The Second Circuit court reversed the decision on appeal, but the defendant in that case has appealed again. Other circuit courts (the fifth and the eleventh) have meanwhile ruled *against* Title VII offering protection for sexual orientation. At the time I write these words, the Supreme Court has just agreed to rule on whether Title VII covers sexual orientation, but until it issues a ruling, the ability of LGBTQ individuals to seek legal redress for sexual harassment at work is limited.[14]

Nor does the EEOC always come through, even though its website promises that "Discrimination against an individual because of gender identity, including transgender status, or because of sexual orientation is discrimination because of sex in violation of Title VII." For example, in 2018 the EEOC dismissed Jeffrey Willy's complaint against his former employer, Eli Lilly and Company, although this case is still pending in the US District Court for the Southern District of Indiana. Willy, a research scientist who is gay, says he faced years of retaliation after complaining to HR about a toxic work environment, including an incident in which his supervisor told him outright, "I hate fags. Well, not all fags, just the flamboyant ones."[15]

Yet even if the legal system is inadequate, companies must still act to ensure that LGBTQ individuals—like all other individuals, gay and straight, male and female, people of color and Caucasian—can flourish in the workplace. As we shall see in later chapters of this book, collaboration and innovation does not happen unless all members of a team feel confident that they will be fairly rewarded and equally respected. That is what inclusion is all about. There is no room in this equation for sexual abuse.

Abusive cultures not only damage individuals but also the organizations that employ them. As I'll explore in the next chapter, Kamran's story is a cautionary tale: when individuals suffer harassment and assault they vote with their feet—and put their companies at a grave disadvantage in the war for top talent.

6

HITS TO THE BOTTOM LINE

When the #MeToo movement caught fire in late 2017, rather few business leaders were seriously concerned. For sure, the press reports were lurid and distressing, but the prevailing view was that the scandals would blow over; #MeToo was a passing squall. A year later the mood in the C-Suite was quite different. In March of 2019, Bradford Hu, Citigroup's chief risk officer, told me, "All boards are thinking about it, and not just in financial services. It could be a strategic risk."

Boards of directors are paying attention to sexual misconduct, because it's not only individuals who pay a heavy price for harassment and assault—whether deservedly, as perpetrators are forced out amid scandal, or tragically, as victims who see careers and lives upended. The organizations that harbor predators pay a price, too, and they usually keep paying for years.

Ongoing legal expenses, the loss of key rainmakers, and a crashing share price are just the beginning. Sexual scandals can also cause companies to lose what is the biggest battle for many: the war for talent. Misconduct and its aftermath poison the workplace environment, driving out employees, crippling recruiting, destroying sponsor–protégé relationships, and denying opportunities to those whom the organization needs most. The hit to the brand, whether internally (among employees) or externally (among recruits, consumers, and investors) can also be devastating. Companies, cultural institutions, nonprofit organizations, government agencies, and political parties can even face questions about their very legitimacy.

In addition, we'll look at the proven steps that organizations such as Citi have taken to minimize the risks and the damage that sexual misconduct can cause to all of their stakeholders. But first, let's better understand that damage. There are five main ways in which sexual misconduct can hit the bottom line.

HIT #1: LAWYERS AND SETTLEMENTS

What is one of the first things that experienced leaders think when they hear of sexual misconduct in the ranks? That it's time to break out the checkbook, because the organization is going to have to pay. Consider Michigan State University, where a staff doctor, Larry Nassar, assaulted and abused young gymnasts for years. When we add together not just the settlements to the young women, but fines and lawyers' fees, the total legal costs to MSU could be more than $1 billion.[1] The Catholic Church, which for decades looked the other way as clergymen sexually abused young people, has so far had to pay more than $3 billion in settlements in the United States alone.[2]

Corporations, too, pay and pay, then pay some more, when executives turn out to be predators. Legal settlements are rarely "one and done." In the fiscal year that ended in June 2017, for example, Twenty-First Century Fox first paid $50 million to settle sexual harassment and discrimination allegations in its Fox News division. Then the company paid another $65 million to the accused senior executives to oust them from the company.[3] Then the company paid $10 million more in 2018 to settle yet another round of allegations.[4] Pension funds and other shareholders, meanwhile, sued Fox's directors and managers over their failed oversight and won an additional $90 million.[5]

Fox News is perhaps the most prominent example, but other companies have also faced serious legal costs as a result of sexual misconduct. Google paid $135 million to get rid of two executives credibly accused of sexual misconduct.[6] Google is also facing an employee lawsuit over sexual harassment and a "bro culture,"[7] while both a major investor and several pension funds are suing the board of Google's parent company, Alphabet, for having damaged the company's value "by covering up sexual abuse by senior executives."[8] To take just a few more examples among well-known companies, the fashion company Guess recently paid half a million dollars in settlements over sexual misconduct allegations—with lawyers' fees likely adding significantly to that sum.[9] At about the same time, Vice Media quietly paid off four women who accused executives of sexual harassment, assault, or retaliation—and then faced a major public relations scandal.[10]

In many cases, it can be difficult to measure the exact size of the legal costs, since so many are settled out of court, discreetly. But the sums involved can be astonishingly high. In 2012, a federal jury ordered a hospital—not an organization with deep pockets like Google or Fox News—to pay a physician's assistant $168 million for sexual harassment that she had suffered repeatedly over several years.[11] Although the parties subsequently reached a settlement for an undisclosed amount that is presumably less than that $168 million, the total cost to the hospital, including legal fees, surely was enough to make that institution's finances shudder.

The Legal Risks Are Rising in the United States

The US government's statistics show that more and more employees who allege sexual harassment are taking legal action and seeking redress from their employers. Preliminary numbers from the EEOC indicate a 12 percent increase in the number of sexual harassment charges filed and a 50 percent increase in lawsuits alleging sexual harassment in 2018 compared to 2017.[12]

For organizations that lack strong, effective policies against sexual harassment and assault, the direct legal and financial risks are growing.

Many cases that cost companies significant sums never reach a jury or the public eye. Between 2010 and 2015—before the #MeToo movement caught fire—employers paid out $699 million to employees alleging sexual harassment just through one of many possible channels for such payments: the Equal Employment Opportunity Commission's administrative enforcement pre-litigation process.[13] Many instances of sexual misconduct are swept under the rug, through "binding arbitration" or simply because victims are afraid to speak up. In those cases, the damage to the company is more indirect, as we'll see. But one of the salutary results of #MeToo has been a rise in victims who are willing to speak out and fight back.

There is a further, indirect legal cost, too: incidents of sexual misconduct, by indicating that a supervisor has a biased state of mind, "may not amount to a harassment claim," law professor Elizabeth Tapscott recently wrote, "but they are a smoking gun in a later discrimination claim."[14] In other words, even if the harassment itself does not become a direct legal liability for the company, it can serve as supporting evidence for lawsuits alleging discrimination. Those can be extraordinarily expensive.

Consider a currently ongoing lawsuit against investment bank Goldman Sachs, alleging sexual discrimination. The plaintiff's complaint is over the unfair distribution of promotions and bonuses—but its evidence begins, as is common in such cases, with an accusation of the plaintiff's then boss kissing and groping her and requesting sex. It was only after she turned him down, the plaintiff alleges, that she began to suffer professionally. This case recently won class-action status, turning it into a potentially giant liability for the Wall Street giant.[15]

Such legal threats to companies are confirmation that, as Professor Tapscott recently wrote in the *Minnesota Law Review*, "Harassment, previously viewed as a contained liability, has morphed into a bet-the-company risk."[16]

The Global Risks Are Rising, Too

The #MeToo movement began in the United States, and US jurisprudence has been one of the leaders in holding individuals and companies responsible for misconduct, but the risks to organizations and careers extend far beyond the borders of the United States. In the United Kingdom, professional services giant Deloitte recently fired twenty partners for "sexual harassment and bullying." For a firm such as Deloitte, its partners create the business and embody the brand. Losing twenty is a big hit. In Australia, Deloitte's rivals EY and KPMG have also lost key leaders to sexual harassment allegations.[17]

A Japanese company, Mitsubishi, in 1989 had to pay a

then record $34 million to settle a sexual harassment lawsuit stemming from managers' misconduct at a plant in Illinois.[18] Inside Japan, that country's Supreme Court recently affirmed the punishment of two men in managerial positions at the Osaka Aquarium for sexually harassing women.[19] An article in the *National Law Review* called this decision from Japan's top court "noteworthy," since it "recognized purely verbal sexual harassment as a punishable offense" and "opens up the potential [in Japan] to implement meaningful penalties for verbal harassment in the workplace."[20]

France, too, has been having a #MeToo movement. Although "cultural resistance" to combating sexual harassment may be stronger there than in the United States,[21] the country recently saw four women and one man win a major sexual harassment case against one of the country's largest cleaning companies.[22] The total fines that the company had to pay, about €220,000, may be modest by US standards, but legal fees surely added to that, and the precedent is important. If even poorly compensated immigrant cleaning staff can successfully sue a major French company for having tolerated sexual harassment, other French companies will have to be on guard, too.

In Brazil, one of that country's leading soap opera stars, José Mayer, has seen his career crash after a costume designer reported him for harassing and groping her. After other women came forward, the country's dominant media company, Globo, severed its contract with Mayer and forbid its directors and scriptwriters to cast him in any future productions.[23]

From aquariums in Osaka to accounting firms in London, train stations in Paris, and TV studios in Rio de Janeiro, the message is clear: the rules have changed. Companies can no longer turn a blind eye to sexual misconduct in their workplaces.

HIT #2: THE LOSS OF KEY LEADERS
AND RAINMAKERS

Some men and women truly have an illness—they cannot control their sexual behavior. But it seems likely such illness is rare in the highest ranks of corporate America. On the contrary, I would argue, those personalities who rise to the top tend to display qualities of shrewd decision-making and strong self-discipline. They carefully weigh risks and incentives.

If this hypothesis is correct, then it would be untrue to say that most leaders whom we have seen display predatory behavior "can't help it." On the contrary, most predators acted as they did because the organizational environment and culture made them think (correctly, until recently) that they could get away with it. Had the environment been different, these leaders—who may be superlative performers—might have kept their abusive tendencies under control. They might still today be at their posts, making it rain, delivering top numbers, and leading their organizations to one success after another.

Companies should be especially attentive to the need for policies that inhibit and punish sexual misconduct among men and women in power, due to the nature of power itself. We've all heard the saying that "power corrupts," but as we've seen in the pages of this book, power corrupts in particularly corrosive ways when it intersects with sex, lust, and hierarchy. "Sexual Overperception," an academic study mentioned in chapter 3, states its main takeaway clearly: "Power motivates heightened perceptions and expectations of sexual interest from subordinates."[24]

In other words, if a previously harmless and respectful person rises to a position of authority over those whom he or she considers sexually attractive, that person will often begin to take advantage of that power to demand sexual favors. He or she may even consider it his or her "right" to do so. And, as discussed in chapters 3 and 4, organizational traditions may even *encourage* previously well-behaved employees to engage in sexual harassment and abuse, by presenting it as a tool to establish one's membership of the superior group that comprises the leadership circle.[25]

It is a trap that companies must watch out for: even men or women with no history of sexual misconduct may become a danger to those beneath them once they achieve a position of power. And if they have risen on their merits, and their employers then find themselves obliged to dismiss these high performers for misconduct, these employers will take a big hit. We need not feel sympathy for predators in power to recognize that the organizations that lose their talents often face a major loss in performance and a costly period of uncertainty. The most prominent example is of course the man whose crimes finally brought #MeToo into the public eye, Harvey Weinstein. After losing the man who was called Hollywood's "King Midas," the company (see below) became "officially dead."[26]

When the Damage Includes Bankruptcy

Amid the sordid details of Harvey Weinstein's sexual crimes—at least eighty-seven women have accused him of misconduct[27]—it may be easy to lose track of a key fact: the women he abused, who typically suffered either massive damage to their careers, lasting personal trauma, or both, were not his only victims.

The company he founded and led, the Weinstein Company, filed for bankruptcy in March 2018. In covering the filing, the

New York Times specifically cited the need for bankruptcy proceedings to "halt an array of lawsuits against the company, including those filed by women who contend that the studio facilitated misconduct by Mr. Weinstein."[28] Naturally, without Harvey Weinstein, the Weinstein Company also lost its ability to attract projects and talent.

That was a huge piece of collateral damage, because Weinstein was for many years Hollywood's "King Midas": the films he produced received more than three hundred Oscar nominations; his hits included *The English Patient*, *Shakespeare in Love*, *Pulp Fiction*, *The Crying Game*, and *The King's Speech*; and he had a track record of turning both directors and actors into celebrities. "He is the gatekeeper to getting projects made, getting your face on screen, to you getting an Oscar," one director said in 2017.[29]

Without Weinstein, the company that bore his name simply had no reason to be, so it died out; but more than a hundred employees depended directly on that company for their livelihood—and then there are all the directors, film crews, actors, and subcontractors who will no longer receive opportunities and employment from a company that has ceased to exist. There are also, perhaps, great films that will now never be made. It is now clear that the Weinstein Company was rotten at its core, yet it was an extraordinary engine for growth and success in an industry that sorely needs such engines.

Many great films will still get made, and many of the talented people who had received work and contracts from the Weinstein Company will land on their feet. But the sudden loss of a company that created great jobs and produced world-class films underscores the damage done by sexual misconduct.

Les Moonves richly deserved to lose his job as CEO of media giant CBS after numerous women accused him of sexual harassment, and after evidence emerged that he may have destroyed the careers of women who turned down his advances. But the fact remains that, in losing Moonves, CBS lost a leader who led the network from last to first in the Neilson ratings, steered it through the 2008 global financial crisis, and then found new sources of revenue to replace the structural decline in TV advertising revenue.[30]

Moonves evidently lacks a moral compass, but he is a talented executive. A different company, with a different culture, might well have been able to benefit from his talents without enabling his flaws. Instead, CBS senior executives and members of the board appear to have condoned—even encouraged—his bad behavior by engaging in "an active cover-up" that lasted for years. The result was that sexual misconduct was not nipped in the bud, but rather spread, finally leading to "a disaster for CBS shareholders."[31]

Examples of toxic leadership cultures, rife with cover-ups, extend far beyond the media world. Consider, for example, perhaps the most important part of the US economy today, technology. A key Silicon Valley player, Dave McClure, had to resign from the start-up incubator 500 Startups that he had founded after multiple accusations of misconduct. Another key partner in that same firm, a woman, then resigned, too—not because she was guilty of misconduct, but out of outrage at how the company "had covered up a separate harassment episode." Another Silicon Valley venture capital firm, Binary Capital, collapsed in an "implosion" after women reported that its founder, Justin Caldbeck, pressed them for sexual favors while they were seeking funding for their firm.[32]

Yet another tech-oriented VC firm, DFJ, lost its founding partner, Steven Jurvetson (a member of Tesla's board, among others), after accusations of "predatory behavior."[33] Top venture capitalist (and early investor in Uber) Shervin Pishevar had to resign from the firm he founded, Sherpa Capital, after six women accused him of sexual misconduct.[34] And Fidelity Investments had to fire its star technology fund manager, Gavin Baker, responsible for more than $16 billion in investments, after he, too, was accused of sexual harassment.[35]

No industry is immune from this danger. To take just one more particularly spectacular example, apparel giant Nike (see page 112) lost the heart of its leadership team—eleven senior executives, including the CEO's heir apparent—to allegations of sexual misconduct.[36]

HIT #3: COLLAPSING MARKET VALUATIONS

When engineer Susan Fowler published her now famous blog post on sexual harassment and cover-up at the ridesharing giant Uber, she set off a firestorm.[37] After her post, many other women at Uber came forward, forcing an investigation that laid bare a toxic workplace culture riddled with bias, bullying, and sexual misconduct. The Uber board eventually fired CEO Travis Kalanick—who cofounded the company—along with twenty other executives and paid out $10 million in settlements.[38]

Ten million dollars is real money for most of us, but perhaps not for a privately held company that, prior to Fowler's post, was valued at $68 billion. But within four months of Fowler's blog post, Uber's share price on the private secondary market fell as much as 15 percent—the equivalent of a $10 billion loss in market capitalization, according to *Fortune*.[39] A few months later, the company's valuation had fallen further, adding up to a $20 billion loss in value.[40]

Uber at the time certainly faced other challenges. Not all of its loss in shareholder value was due to its toxic culture. But *Fortune* listed the scandal over sexual misconduct as among the top reasons for the hit to valuation, and the influential technology news website Recode described Fowler as having "brought Uber to its knees."[41]

Since then, Uber's valuation has more than recovered, and it went public in a giant IPO. Yet that IPO was generally considered a "disappointment," with shares priced below expectations and then immediately dropping 8 percent on the first day of trading.[42] We cannot know what precise effect the sexual misconduct scandals had on this result, but the fact is that for nearly a year, sexual misconduct shaved several billion dollars off this giant company's valuation—and after its new CEO, Dara Khosrowshahi, took the helm, he had to spend a large proportion of his valuable time not focusing on growing revenue and profits, but in "damage-control mode" dealing with "an epic-scale mess."[43] Khosrowshahi has made excellent efforts in this respect (and I'll look at these efforts in chapter 10), but changing the culture has been a lengthy, strenuous effort that is still ongoing.[44]

Even more clear-cut than the case of Uber is the damage that Wynn Resorts, a publicly traded company, suffered after the *Wall Street Journal* revealed that dozens of women were accusing its CEO, Steve Wynn, of misconduct, and that Wynn had paid $7.5 million to settle one such incident.[45] The day the *Journal*'s story ran, the stock price of Wynn Resorts fell 8 percent. The next trading day, shares fell another 9 percent, wiping a total of $3.5 billion off the company's valuation.[46]

Wynn finally resigned, but the financial bloodletting has continued.[47] As I write these words, the company is worth $8 billion less than it was before Wynn's misconduct came to light. Wynn was the face and the business brain behind the company that bore his name. Additionally, since many casinos have "moral clauses" attached to gaming licenses, there has been concern that his misconduct may impair the company's ability to operate going forward. Wynn Resorts has been able to expand with a new casino in the Boston area, though not without first paying a $35 million fine to the Massachusetts Gaming Commission for failure to disclose the sexual misconduct charges in the application for a license.

Seven and a half million dollars may have been pocket change for Wynn; perhaps it was even covered by insurance. But $8 billion is most certainly a heavy price for Wynn Resorts shareholders to pay.

Other examples include nearly every publicly traded company that has suffered a scandal over sexual misconduct. CBS shares, for example, fell more than 6 percent the day the story of Les Moonves's misconduct broke.[48] It is therefore no surprise that a growing source of costly lawsuits over sexual misconduct (such as those against Google and Fox News, mentioned previously) is investor anger over the impact on share price. As a recent article in Law360 put it, "Investors Say 'Us Too' in Wake of Sexual Misconduct Claims."[49]

HIT #4: DRAINING THE TALENT PIPELINE

"I am in the midst of recruiting for a very important role on my team," Bradford Hu, Citi's chief risk officer, says. "The new person would be a direct report to me. I just interviewed an amazing female professional who works at another bank. And she brought up, on her own, that we would be an employer of choice for her, as a woman. She said that one of the reasons she was talking to

Citigroup is because we are more diverse in senior management than our competitors, and we have stated goals and a commitment to progressing women to the top ranks of the organization." That's a big win for Citi—but what happens at companies that do not welcome women and other diverse individuals? According to Hu, the threat to such companies can be "existential," especially in an industry such as financial services, where talent is "the most important resource."

Talent is indeed the most important resource for more and more companies today, and female talent has been almost entirely overlooked in some sectors. In the notoriously inhospitable hedge fund world, for example, as recently as 2018 less than 20 percent of all employees were women—yet according to a 2015 study by Northeastern University, hedge funds run by women tend to perform better than those run by men.[50] In technology, another sector where women often feel unwelcome, a search for top talent often includes a bidding war. The costs associated with both finding talent and losing talent can be staggering. In 2017, on the eve of the #MeToo movement's explosion into public consciousness, the Kapor Center published a study on why people *left* jobs at tech companies. Such departures, the Kapor Center estimated, cost US tech companies $16 billion.

The top reason for voluntary departures? It was not compensation, but *culture*. Two thirds of those who voluntarily left their tech jobs said that they would have stayed if their employer had fixed its culture. Some of the more hard-hitting criticisms came from female employees. One in ten of the women who participated in this survey reported unwanted sexual attention, a quarter reported being passed over for a deserved promotion, and one in six had encountered negative assumptions about their ability. According to one Latina engineer, "My CEO clearly lacked respect for women . . . He made sexual remarks about women in front of female employees during off-sites . . . and when accused of micromanaging women he said point blank that he lacked trust in their abilities. After I left, all of the other women quit, too."[51]

The damage done by toxic cultures doesn't stop at women. When sexual misconduct runs unchecked, the damage spreads from the victims to their colleagues and the broader workplace environment. As the data in chapter 2 shows, when men hear of sexual harassment occurring at work, their reported job satisfaction falls to 43 percent from 56 percent. While both men and women report a 25 percent falloff in their dedication and commitment when they know that their boss is having an affair with a subordinate.

Even if you personally do not suffer harassment, when you witness your supervisor pressuring your coworker for sex, and when you see top management turn a blind eye, it changes your opinion of the company and of your place and future in it. Various questions start running through your head.

Are supervisors really making decisions on assignments and promotions (or firings) based on merit? Will you only stand a chance at rising if you are sexually attractive and available to your superiors? If you hold a closed-door meeting with a superior with a reputation for harassment, are you at risk? Should you perhaps avoid such meetings, even though cultivating strong relationships with superiors is one of the best ways to rise in any organization? And if you do get a promotion, will your coworkers suspect you of having slept your way to the top?

Such are the questions employees are likely to ask at firms where sexual predators roam freely, and such questions can lead to low morale, disengagement, and flight risk. To take an example, in October 2018, twenty thousand (mostly male) Google employees held a walkout to protest sexual harassment, sexual misconduct, and a noninclusive workplace culture at the technology giant.[52] That is surely evidence of a morale problem at a company currently engaged in a war to attract and retain top tech talent.

Yet there is another, perhaps bigger problem that particularly impacts high-achieving women and other underrepresented groups: the hit to sponsor–protégé relationships that cross the lines of gender and other divides. "Where sexual harassment is tolerated," says Ricardo Anzaldua, general counsel at Freddie Mac (which has a zero-tolerance policy), "you will find many good guys just running for the exits when it comes to sponsoring women. Because it's often too dangerous for them to be seen as advocates for women." Sponsorship—a senior colleague taking a top junior talent under his or her wing as a protégé and advocating for opportunities and recognition—is perhaps the most critical lever for a young high achiever to rise to the top. It is especially critical for women, people of color, and LGBTQ individuals, who often lack membership in the old boys' clubs that dominate the inner circles of power.[53]

Without sponsorship for women, there will be very few female leaders at a company. And without women leaders, a company will be at a severe competitive disadvantage. Several highly regarded studies from Catalyst,[54] McKinsey,[55] Credit Suisse,[56] Bloomberg,[57] and Morgan Stanley[58] demonstrate that a "critical mass" of women around decision-making tables (in the C-suite and on boards of directors) enhances a company's ROI. Additionally, there is a positive impact on innovation and new market growth. CTI's research report *Innovation, Diversity, and Market Growth* found that companies that have achieved a significant degree of diversity in leadership are far less likely to report problems with "groupthink" (25 percent vs 40 percent) and far more likely to have executives willing to see value in ideas that they personally don't see a need for (62 percent vs 37 percent).[59]

This same CTI study found that, on a team level, when a team had at least one member that mirrored the identity of the end-user demographic, 61 percent of the team reported a better understanding of the target demographic. When teams lacked this representation, only 25 percent of the team said that they understood the target demographic.[60] So when either sexual misconduct, or the suspicion it leaves in its wake, squeezes women—and other diverse cohorts—out of the talent pipeline, a company's ability to innovate and reach new markets suffers.

Clearly, if men harass and assault women to make their subordinate role clear, they are not grooming them as leaders. Strangely, the #MeToo movement—which is all about ridding the workplace of such sexual misconduct—has itself become a drag on female progression, at least in the short run. *New York Times* columnist Nicholas Kristof has remarked on the "many male bosses saying in surveys that they are less willing now [after #MeToo] to mentor junior female colleagues, go to dinner with them, travel with them—to generally treat them as coworkers rather than as land mines."[61] A nationally representative survey found that 60 percent of women fear that #MeToo could deny women professional opportunities, because men—fearful of accusations and rumors—are now reluctant to work with them.[62] It was even a subject that emerged at the World Economic Forum in Davos, a gathering spot for many of the world's most powerful people: several male leaders there said that, due to #MeToo, they are now afraid to spend one-on-one time with young women in their organizations.[63]

But, as Ricardo Anzaldua noted, the fundamental problem is

not publicity around sexual misconduct. The problem is sexual misconduct. If men and women are working together in an environment where there is no room for assault, harassment, and bullying, there will be no fear of either being a victim or of being falsely accused of inappropriate behavior. So if a company wishes to effectively recruit, retain, and support the rise of talented men and women up the pipeline, as well as ensure that talented women receive the same opportunities for mentorship and sponsorship that men do, it will have to make the fight against sexual misconduct (for which this book's last chapter offers guidance) a priority.

HIT #5: DAMAGE TO THE BRAND

"From a brand reputation risk perspective, you need to invest in a thorough program." That's what Diane Gherson, chief human resources officer at IBM, said, when I asked her about the biggest risk to companies from sexual misconduct in their ranks. "The cost can be devastating," she continued. "And it's very hard to recover from a brand threat associated with a credible charge of sexual harassment. With social media, a shared photo, video, or blog post can go viral. And no one can dispute it."

How much is a company's brand worth? If you're Apple, it's worth well north of $100 billion, according to *Forbes*.[64] Most companies' brands aren't worth billions, but for all companies, their brand is—by its very nature—what defines them with consumers, investors, current and future employees, and business partners. Research shows that Gherson is spot-on: sexual harassment or assault can do a lot of damage to a brand very quickly.

A study conducted by UCLA's Anderson School of Management, published in the *Harvard Business Review* and reported in the

Washington Post, indicated that even a *single* instance of sexual harassment is enough to "dramatically reduce public perceptions of an entire organization's gender equity."[65] The study also notes that "individuals are more prone to attribute a sexual harassment claim to a hostile organizational culture than they are to perceive it as a single, 'bad apple' manager" and that people "were more likely to generalize a sexual harassment claim to the organizational culture than a financial fraud claim."[66] In other words, just one incident of sexual harassment or assault is enough to contaminate an entire organization in the eyes of many.

It is difficult to put a precise number to the financial hit caused when a sexual scandal damages a company's brand, but for consumer-facing companies, it is surely gigantic. A company such as Lululemon, for example, did not become a multibillion-dollar company by selling yoga pants. It became a phenomenon by selling women an image of health, beauty, empowerment, and self-esteem. What happens to that image when women see newspaper headlines such as "Suit Claims Lululemon Worker Raped by Boss after Company Created 'Perfect Environment' for Sex Predator?" How about when women dig deeper into the article, to learn that female workers at Lululemon were "ostracized" for "not wearing revealing enough clothes" or that staff "slapped each other's asses" to mock videos meant to combat sexual harassment?[67]

One doesn't need to be a branding expert to know that the damage is severe, but an actual branding expert, Beanstalk's Michael Stone, spelled it out in a *Forbes* column: "That kind of misconduct by senior executives of any company is horribly off message and the brand's reputation is tarnished. And not only is the brand damaged but other parties are damaged as well, such as retailers and licensees." For employees, too, Stone writes, the hit to the brand has severe repercussions: "Retention becomes more challenging. Respect deteriorates. Morale falls. Performance is affected."[68] Along with Lululemon, Nike, too (see page 112), has surely taken a hit to its brand among female consumers from evidence that inside the company women were "devalued and demeaned."[69]

The impact of sexual misconduct on reputation and brand extends beyond the corporate world. Who can think the same of the Catholic Church after so many reports have emerged of the church hierarchy protecting predatory priests? In late 2018, for example, a grand jury in Pennsylvania found evidence that at least three hundred priests had abused more than one thousand children. In the words of the grand jury report, "Priests were raping little boys and girls, and the men of God who were responsible for them not only did nothing; they hid it all. For decades."[70] Clearly, an institution that has as one of its reasons for existence the protection of the vulnerable—especially children—will face a crisis of legitimacy over such abuse. A recent *Washington Post* article noted that the Catholic Church has lost more members than any other religion in the last decades, with the sex scandals cited as the main reason by almost half of those who have left the church. "It's almost unsalvageable. The church is in pieces. People have completely separated their faith from the organization," the president of a Catholic university told the *Washington Post.*[71]

Other examples abound, in and out of the private sector. A venerable charity in London, the Presidents Club, that funded hospitals and auctioned off events such as tea with the governor of the Bank of England, was forced to shut down after media reports emerged of donors groping young hostesses at a charity dinner.[72] One of the world's largest fast fashion chains, Topshop, was hit by a Twitter-driven boycott after its founder, Philip Green, was credibly accused of harassing women. Like many "old boys" caught up in scandal, Green allegedly tried to buy the women's silence and sue newspapers into submission. But in the days of #MeToo and social media, silence proved impossible, and the company is taking a hit. "Unless the claims are proven, beyond all doubt, to be false, then there is no coming back," one leading retail analyst said about Topshop and Philip Green. "Quite rightly, the stench of sexual misconduct lingers for life. The sexual abuse of women is not something people forgive or forget, and it will weigh on people's minds when they decide where to shop."[73]

I mentioned Joe Biden earlier, but one of his main political rivals in 2019—Senator Bernie Sanders—also saw his personal and political brand take a hit from accusations of sexual misconduct in the organization that he led. After several women said that they had suffered harassment and discrimination when working on his 2016 presidential campaign, Sanders had to apologize publicly.[74] No one accused Sanders himself of any misconduct or even of knowing about such misconduct at the time it occurred. But his brand has still suffered from having failed to ensure a respectful workplace environment, where both men and women can work free from fear of sexual harassment or assault.

LOOKING FOR ANSWERS

Given the hefty and burgeoning costs associated with sexual harassment and assault, it's not surprising that most organizations and many leaders feel the need for urgent action. Next, I will offer proven action steps that individuals and organizations can take to both staunch the drain of value and move into a much more inclusive future.

A Giant Pays a Giant Price

Nike is by some measures the world's most successful apparel company. Its stock market value is more than $120 billion, and its quarterly revenue routinely exceeds $9 billion. Yet Nike also stands out in another, less fortunate way: the company has suffered, in rapid succession, multiple hits to the bottom line from sexual misconduct in its leadership ranks.

After suffering for years in silence, women at Nike revolted in 2018. They documented incidents of misconduct—including forcible kisses and supervisors e-mailing women about their breasts—and of discrimination in promotions and assignments. Women also documented having complained to HR without finding any recourse.[75]

When they finally went to the CEO and to the public, the company suffered Hit #2: a loss of key leaders and rainmakers. Eleven senior leaders, including the president of the Nike brand who had been seen as the CEO's successor, were forced to resign. This personnel change created uncertainty around the company's future, as a financial analyst told the *New York Times*: "We haven't before seen the exit of people like this who have been there for a very, very long time," the analyst said, "and the question is, are the people who are replacing them ready to take on these new jobs?"[76]

The company is also suffering from Hit #1: legal costs. Both shareholders and former employees are suing Nike— with the possibility of hundreds more women joining the latter lawsuit, according to the plaintiffs' lawyers.[77] A closer look at the company culture also reveals, as is so often the case, that tolerance of misconduct has become ingrained and is likely creating Hit #4: an emptying out of the female talent pipeline.

Women, it turns out, are nearly half the company's workforce, they hold 38 percent of director-level positions, and are 29 percent of vice presidents.[78] These figures aren't good, and they're sliding as the scandals unfold. This is a problem. CTI research (see Hit #4 and discussion in chapter 9) has shown that the presence of women around decision-making tables is crucial for teams to understand female consumers and grow market share among them. A growing paucity of women in leadership at Nike is therefore likely to exacerbate a growing challenge. As the *New York Times* has noted: "Nike is struggling to get traction in women's categories, the fastest-growing segment of the market."[79]

Finally, there's Hit #5. The company is suffering a hit to its most valuable asset: its brand. "'Women Are Devalued and Demeaned' at Nike," screamed a headline at CNN.[80] "Inside Nike, a Boys-Club Culture," the *Wall Street Journal* trumpeted.[81] "Women at Nike Fight Hostile Culture," proclaimed Inc.com.[82] It is hard to measure the precise damage such headlines cause, but when one considers just how much Nike's brand is worth—$32 billion, according to *Forbes*[83]—it is clear that the potential cost is huge.

Shareholders certainly think that these costs are significant (Hit #3). When a shareholders' group filed a lawsuit against Nike's management in late 2018 over their handling of sexual harassment inside the company, they specifically cited a "hostile work environment that has now harmed, and threatens to further tarnish and impair (Nike's) financial position, as well as its reputation and goodwill."[84]

WHAT TO DO

7

LEGAL REMEDIES

Laws are a powerful barometer of what society views as acceptable or unacceptable. Just consider (as chapter 1 shows) how long it took for sexual misconduct to become illegal. Today, in the #MeToo era, both the law and its enforcement are evolving and legal scholars and policymakers have work to do. Clearly, legal measures alone can't do everything, otherwise discrimination in our society would have ended with the Civil Rights Act of 1964. To stamp out sexual misconduct, and the risks it brings to both employees and employers, companies and organizations will also need a talent strategy that emphasizes inclusivity and diversity.

But the law can still be a key part of creating a workplace where everyone can work in an environment of safety and respect. The right legal framework provides both potent protections and a road map that can guide deeper organizational change and better individual behavior.

This chapter looks at the legal remedies in place and where they are going.

THE PAIN OF LAWSUITS AND
THE SILENCE OF ARBITRATION

Here's a situation that is all too common. Your boss invites you out for a drink to discuss a plum assignment, then begins to paw you and says, "If you want the job, come to my hotel room and we'll seal the deal . . ." You say no. The next day he gives the assignment to someone else and announces that he's demoting you.

You might think that you have an airtight case: sexual misconduct followed by retaliation. In the era of #MeToo, with daily revelations in the press of this kind of behavior, you might also think that if you file a lawsuit, the judges and jury will believe you. If you thought all that, of course, you might be right—but you very well might be wrong, and the pain along the way might be devastating.

Consider when, in September 2018, Christine Blasey Ford testified before the Senate Judiciary Committee. Ford told senators (and the nation) that Supreme Court nominee Brett Kavanaugh had assaulted her at a party back in high school. Kavanaugh's powerful allies—Republican senators, backed by the president of the United States, brought in a prosecutor (Rachel Mitchell) not to question Kavanaugh, but to grill Ford. Like most people in such cases, Ford had no witnesses (how many bosses offer assignments in return for sex in front of colleagues?), or at least none willing to testify in public. She did have therapists' notes from years before, saying Kavanaugh's assault of her had contributed to Ford's struggle with anxiety and PTSD. But the prosecutor focused on the word "contributed" and questioned how severe Ford's trauma had been. She also noted that Ford's fear of flying hadn't stopped her from taking a plane to Washington to testify, and that Ford had not elected to have a forensic interview designed for trauma survivors.

This attack played out on national television with millions watching, the prosecutor trying every which way to show that Ford's testimony was politically motivated. As we all know, Ford's courageous stance came to naught: furious and affronted, Kavanaugh denied all charges, Republican senators lined up behind him, and he was duly confirmed to the Supreme Court. Ford's pain did not end there. Death threats rained in and she and her family were forced to move four times and hire a private security detail. Shaken to the core, Ford took an indefinite leave of absence from her job.

Now, not every sexual misconduct case becomes a pawn in an ugly, high-stakes political struggle, but if the men seeking to destroy Ford were also seeking to make an example of her, they succeeded.

Daniela Nanau, an employment and civil rights lawyer in New York who has represented many plaintiffs in sexual misconduct cases, told me in an interview about the chilling effect of the Kavanaugh hearings. "I had two women executives who were potential clients—separate cases. Both had strong evidence that they'd been sexually harassed. But both saw what Dr. Ford was subjected to and pulled out. They said they just couldn't do this. They couldn't subject themselves and their families to that kind of treatment."

Unfortunately, Nanau's clients may have been right to be afraid. Even without the victim getting grilled on national television, things often get ugly when a victim takes an employer to court. It's standard practice for the employer—oftentimes a defendant with deep pockets—to bring on a team of attorneys who will dig through the minutiae of the plaintiff's life. They'll drag the accuser through the mud, seeking any possible evidence that she/he is unstable or invited sexual attention or was failing at her/his job and looking for someone to blame—anything to dilute or discredit the allegation of sexual abuse.

In other words, unless you have never flirted with a colleague, never received a subpar performance rating, or never sought counseling or psychiatric help, you may think twice about seeking recourse for sexual harassment or even assault. As Nanau puts it, "As a society, we have to do better than this."

Paradoxically, however, the way to do things better seems to lie partly in making sure all sexual harassment victims have the option of suing in court—which, at present, they don't.

SUNLIGHT IS THE BEST DISINFECTANT

Painful though they may be, court cases make problems public and can set precedents for future cases. When faced with a lawsuit, employers may agree to settle to avoid the expense and embarrassment of a trial. And if enough cases become public in a given workplace, revealing a pattern of sexual misconduct, victims might be able to file a class action suit.

But for all these options to be open to victims, they must be able to sue. Many, in some cases without even realizing it, have signed away that right. Fully 54 percent of nonunion private-sector employees have had to sign mandatory arbitration agreements. These agreements—often buried in the fine print of a lengthy employment contract—stipulate that if employees have a complaint over harassment, abuse, or wrongful termination, they waive the right to sue the company and must instead present the case to an arbitrator.[1] In arbitration, the proceedings, decision, and settlement are all confidential. It sets no legal precedent for similar cases and leads to no public awareness. In addition, arbitration agreements often forbid class action suits. To cap it all off, arbitration is binding, with no opportunity to appeal.

An employee's chances of winning in arbitration are far worse than in court. "Arbitrators have often worked for the company several times, whereas the interaction with the worker is a one-off," says Terri Gerstein, a fellow in the Harvard Law School Labor and Work Life Program. Since the employer usually chooses the arbitrator, the arbitrator might have an incentive to rule in favor of a repeat client.

Cynthia Estlund, a law professor at New York University, has found that most employment disputes subject to mandatory arbitration agreements "simply evaporate before they are even filed." Using data from employment litigation records and the American Arbitration Association, Estlund estimates that approximately 34,000 arbitration cases per year are initiated but never filed. Estlund believes that for most employees, taking the claim to arbitration is not worth it, due to "the dominant power of employers to tweak and tilt the arbitration process to their liking." As a result, she concludes, "It now appears that, by imposing mandatory arbitration on its employees, an employer can ensure that it will face only a minuscule chance of ever having to answer for legal misconduct against employees."[2]

UNINTENDED CONSEQUENCES

This scenario seems to be an unintended consequence of an effort to make employers *more* accountable for discrimination. In 1991, Congress amended the Civil Rights Act in order to (among other provisions) spell out the right of a victim of discrimination to receive *financial* compensation for compensatory and punitive damages—instead of a court simply ordering a defendant to do better in the future and perhaps adopt new training programs. Although the law capped compensatory and punitive damages at $50,000 to $300,000, depending on the size of the organization, there have, of course, been much larger settlements. A court may determine an award based on additional factors, including lost wages and legal fees, and some states and municipalities have statutes that override the cap.

"The idea was that if victims could litigate for monetary damages, they would be more likely to come forward, and that employers might make a greater effort to put a stop to bad behavior if it was costing them," says Nanau.

But the risk of heavy financial damages was also an incentive for employers to insist on mandatory arbitration clauses and non-disclosure agreements. With an NDA, even if the employer has to pay a large settlement, the plaintiff is bound not to ever let anyone know. Such silence doesn't just save the company from a public relations hit. It prevents other victims of misconduct from knowing about such cases to cite them as precedent. Since it was also in 1991 that the Supreme Court upheld (in *Gilmer v. Interstate/Johnson Lane Corp.*) the enforceability of mandatory arbitration agreements, it's no surprise that they subsequently grew so common.[3]

The last two years have seen moves to weaken mandatory arbitration and NDAs, yet efforts are still falling short. While twelve states have passed laws that restrict NDAs in sexual misconduct cases, only one—New Jersey—has gone so far as to make existing agreements unenforceable, so that the victim isn't bound to something he/she signed, perhaps unwittingly, as a condition of employment.[4] Today, with #MeToo, society is evolving, and employers are under pressure to rethink mandatory arbitration and NDAs.

RETHINKING ARBITRATION

In late October 2018, thousands of Google employees walked out to protest the millions paid in exit packages to Google executives accused of sexual harassment. The organizers issued a list of demands—including an end to mandatory arbitration in sexual harassment cases. In response, Google has made arbitration optional for such claims. Microsoft, too, has removed mandatory arbitration clauses from its employment contracts.

One additional piece of encouraging news is that social media has given victims a new platform for publicizing complaints. Even if someone has signed arbitration and nondisclosure agreements, she/he might leak a sexual harassment complaint anonymously online. Of course, the anonymity of online forums can also enable sexual harassment (as in the example of Zahira Kelly-Cabrera in chapter 5), as well as permit malicious, slanderous accusations of misconduct against innocent men and women (a danger I will discuss in chapter 9). But the fact is, in part thanks to social media, sweeping accusations of misconduct under the rug can now backfire, as word of the offense and the cover-up may still come out, hammering a company's reputation and market value. Business leaders are well aware of this new risk, as IBM's CHRO Diane Gherson pointed out in an interview (featured in chapter 9). That is likely why some employers are starting to give employees a choice of arbitration or litigation.

A LEGAL WISH LIST FOR CHANGING TIMES

A coalition of more than thirty organizations, including the ACLU, the Leadership Conference on Civil and Human Rights, and the National Women's Law Center, issued a report in October 2018 calling on Congress to institute measures to fight sexual misconduct in the workplace. The suggested measures include:

- Eliminate mandatory nondisclosure agreements.
- Eliminate mandatory arbitration agreements.
- Extend workplace civil rights protections against harassment and discrimination for all individuals in workplaces with one or more employees. Title VII currently covers only workplaces with fifteen or more employees.
- Strengthen protections for independent contractors, interns, graduate students, and guest workers.
- To break the silence, require employers to regularly disclose or report to a specified federal, state, or local enforcement agency (such as the Securities and Exchange Commission, the EEOC, or a state fair-employment agency) the number of claims, lawsuits, and settlements involving harassment and discrimination involving the employer and the amounts paid in the aggregate to resolve such matters.
- Remove the caps on compensatory and punitive damages (set at $50,000 to $300,000 depending on employer size more than a quarter century ago).
- Address the judicially created "severe or pervasive" liability standard—sometimes referred to as the "one free grope" rule—so as to correct and prevent unduly restrictive interpretations by the courts.

The report also calls for preventive laws mandating effective annual trainings for all supervisors and employees, and for funding of workplace "climate surveys." These surveys assess the prevalence of harassment and discrimination in the workforce and increasingly are an important tool in addressing and preventing workplace violations.[5]

The Benefits of Accountability

Why has the financial services sector been relatively unscathed by the recent wave of sexual misconduct? One reason is the "Uniform Termination Notice for Securities Industry Registration," typically just called the U5 form. If an employee registered with a broker-dealer or registered investment advisor is fired for cause, the U5—filed with the Financial Industry Regulatory Authority (FINRA)—lists the cause. This form then becomes part of an individual's permanent record, which will follow him or her for the rest of their career.

As Bradford Hu explained to me, this acts as a serious deterrent. "If," Hu says, "an individual is fired for unwanted advances toward a female subordinate, he will never work for another financial services organization. Potential employers get to see all of those reasons for past termination, and no one will hire that person. These are powerful consequences for misconduct: not just taking away a person's job, but their future livelihood. And professionals in financial services understand this."

CONGRESS UPGRADES LEGAL PROCESSES

In December 2018, congressional negotiators reached agreement to overhaul the system for punishing sexual misconduct in their ranks. Going forward, members of Congress charged with sexual misconduct will be required to pay out of pocket for at least some court judgments and settlements.[6] (Previously, taxpayers footed the bill.)

In April 2019, legislators proposed legislation—shaped by a coalition of progressive groups led by the ACLU—called the BE HEARD (Bringing an End to Harassment by Enhancing Accountability and Rejecting Discrimination) in the Workplace Act. Its provisions include research on the economic impact of workplace harassment; mandatory reporting on the prevalence of workplace harassment; more access to training about what constitutes harassment and what defines employee rights; an end to mandatory arbitration and nondisclosure agreements; an expansion of civil rights protections to all workers, including independent contractors and interns; strengthened protections against discrimination based on sexual orientation and gender identity; more time to report harassment; legal assistance for low-income workers; no more caps on damages that an employer might be required to pay; and an end to compensation in the form of tips, because waiters and other tipped workers are disproportionately vulnerable to sexual harassment and discrimination by both clients and supervisors.[7] At press time, lead cosponsor Senator Patty Murray (D-WA) and other cosponsors had turned their efforts to building more grassroots support for the act.

STATES AND CITIES ARE MOVING FASTER

Some state legislatures and city governments have been moving faster than Congress to adapt the law to fight sexual misconduct in the workplace. New York, for example, is in the process of enacting sweeping changes that include: extension of protections against sexual harassment and other human rights violations to employees in organizations of all sizes and to independent contractors; lowering the burden of proof so that complainants no longer need to show that harassment is "severe and pervasive"; an end to mandatory arbitration agreements for any cases of discrimination or retaliation; and limits on confidentiality demands.

The National Women's Law Center in Washington, DC, tracks these advances. Here are some examples of specific new protections, updated as of July 2019:[8]

- Three hundred state legislators from forty states have made a commitment to strengthen protections against sexual misconduct in twenty states by 2020.
- Twelve states have limited or prohibited employers from requiring employees to sign NDAs as a condition for employment or as part of a settlement agreement.
- Ten states and New York City have enacted key sexual misconduct prevention measures that include mandatory training.
- Five states have expanded workplace harassment protections to include contractors, interns and graduate students.

Despite this progress and these wins, much work remains. For a start, without congressional action, the risk remains of a federal court overturning state prohibitions against mandatory arbitration. In addition, even if a plaintiff can "freely" choose litigation over arbitration, the incentives to remain silent remain powerful. "If there's an out, the employer will say, we'll award you more money if you keep it all confidential," says Nanau. And although so-called gig-economy workers in New York may soon have recourse, those in the other forty-nine states do not.

A Global Standard?

At the annual conference of the International Labour Organization (ILO) in Geneva in June 2019, delegates adopted a new convention and recommendation to combat violence and harassment in the workplace around the world. The convention recognized violence and harassment in the workplace as a human rights violation and a threat to equal opportunities, and reminds member nations that they have a responsibility to promote a "general environment of zero tolerance."[9]

The convention needs to be ratified by two member states to become a legally binding international instrument. The U.S. is one of 187 member states of the ILO.

LAWS FOR BYSTANDERS

Some local laws are now paying attention to a critical component of cultural change: bystander intervention. For example, Carol Goodman, a partner specializing in sexual misconduct law at the

New York law firm Herrick Feinstein LLP, notes that New York City now requires that companies provide anti–sexual harassment training that includes "a discussion on bystander intervention, including examples of how to engage in bystander intervention."[10]

"Managers have certain obligations already," Goodman says. "Bystander intervention encourages *any* employee who sees something that looks inappropriate to step forward. For example, if you hear a comment from a coworker that may cross the line, say, 'that isn't funny.' If you see a female colleague getting into a cab with a male supervisor and she looks uncomfortable, call her over and ask her to ride with you. She might be in a threatening situation or she might not. Either way, you have just interrupted the situation. An employee can intervene by just e-mailing HR, saying they saw something that didn't look right. HR can look into it and it may be nothing, or something minor. On the other hand, HR might have received another complaint about the same individual. When the complaints are viewed together, the conduct may rise to another level. The point is that bystanders can often intervene, diffuse, or disrupt a situation before it has a chance to escalate."

Goodman's insight is precisely why bystanders can be "upstanders," speeding up cultural change inside an organization, as chapter 9 will show.

FORTY THOUSAND COMPLAINTS A YEAR: THE FEAR OF RETALIATION

"In nearly every case, once a woman went public she faced retaliation." That's what Sharyn Tejani, director of the Time's Up Legal Defense Fund, reports in relation to the nearly four thousand complaints of workplace sexual harassment that the fund received its first year of operation.[11] Retaliation—which may come in the form of firing, demotion, or day-to-day hostility in the workplace—has been, for the last decade, the EEOC's most frequently filed charge. In 2018, the EEOC received nearly forty thousand complaints alleging retaliation: 52 percent of all charges filed. In theory the law protects victims of sexual misconduct from retaliation, enabling them to sue for damages if they suffer retaliation over a complaint; in practice, the threat of retaliation is enough to keep the vast majority of victims silent. According to the EEOC, roughly three out of four victims of harassment never talked to a supervisor, manager, or union representative. They feared not just disbelief but, even more important, retaliation.[12]

Merrick (Rick) Rossein, a professor at the City University of New York Law School, is one of the prominent legal experts working to make the laws forbidding harassment and assault, and forbidding retaliation against complainants, more effective. Rossein has litigated a number of high-profile harassment cases, including the landmark EEOC v. Sage Realty Corporation. In that case, the US District Court for the Southern District of New York upheld a charge of sex discrimination against Margaret Hasselman and awarded compensation. Hasselman's employer had fired her when she refused to wear a sexually revealing outfit known as the "bicentennial uniform" for her job as a lobby attendant in an office building. In her lawsuit, Hasselman said that the uniform created a situation in which she was the target of lewd or obscene propositions and gestures. In the wake of this lawsuit, Rossein came up with a way to prevent victims such as Hasselman from being fired in the first place. He has written a proposal that stipulates that if a company is hit with a sexual harassment suit, the chair of its ethics committee should issue a written anti-retaliation plan, which should be signed by the alleged harasser and (if applicable) a high-level manager, with a copy given to the accuser. Sample language includes the following:

[Name of accused] shall not directly or indirectly take, or directly or indirectly cause anyone else to take, any adverse or retaliatory action of punishment ("Retaliation") against: 1. Any employee, intern or independent contractor because of a complaint lodged under the Employer's Harassment Policy or that person's objection to alleged sexual and/or gender harassment and/or retaliation; or 2. Anyone who speaks with, or otherwise provides information to, the employer or any independent investigation counsel about the complaint ("Witnesses"), because of the Witness' participation in the investigation. 3. Prohibited Retaliation includes, without limitation: a. Directly or indirectly causing any damage to any complainant's reputation or negatively affecting her/his employment and/or professional and/or future opportunities because of her/his assertion of a complaint under the Harassment Policy or her/his objection to alleged sexual harassment and or retaliation; and b. Directly or indirectly causing any damage to the reputation of any Witnesses or negatively affecting any Witness' employment and/or professional and/or future opportunities because of the Witness' participation in the investigation; and c. Directly or indirectly causing a third party to engage in the above-described conduct.[13]

The idea, says Rossein, "is that the company is giving the accused a list of things he can't do, and the target is told that if any retaliatory actions occur, she should tell the investigator." The New York State Assembly has adopted his plan in its Policy Prohibiting Harassment, Discrimination and Retaliation. Rossein is also actively presenting it to other organizations.

It's fascinating to note that Rossein's proposal assumes that in cases of sexual harassment and assault the predator is a male and the prey is a female. His language is unexceptional—even standard—in the law. As earlier chapters of this book make clear, this assumption is inaccurate. Sexual predators include Avital Ronell as well as Charlie Rose, and sexual prey include Joseph Oncale as well as Monica Lewinsky. Legal scholars and the law need to abandon stereotypes and see sex as something that can be weaponized by anyone who has authority and power at work.

A HIGHER STANDARD THAN THE LAW

One day in the summer of 2016, New York State Assemblyman Steven F. McLaughlin said something blatantly inappropriate to a woman on his staff: he asked if he could have nude photos of her. She reported the incident. McLaughlin retaliated, telling the story with graphic details and revealing her name to a former employee who spread juicy tidbits around. The Assembly's Ethics and Guidance Committee investigated and found that McLaughlin had violated policies prohibiting harassment, discrimination, and retaliation. He had also lied to investigators, claiming that he had no idea why she would be complaining about him.

Had this woman taken McLaughlin to court, what would have happened? By the letter of the law, it's possible that the answer is *nothing*. "A court might have ruled that McLaughlin's actions weren't in violation of the law because of the precedent that a hostile work environment has to be severe or pervasive," says Rossein. Fortunately for the plaintiff (and the citizens of New York paying McLaughlin's salary), the Assembly decided to hold its actions "to their own higher standards, above the floor that the law establishes."

The woman did not receive a lucrative settlement, but she also did not have to endure a trial; and though McLaughlin did not lose his job, the Assembly sanctioned him and published a letter of admonition making his guilty behavior public—a significant punishment for an elected official in New York.[14] The sanctions included a recommendation that he reimburse the Assembly out of his own pocket for the "comprehensive supplemental sexual harassment and retaliation prevention training" he had already been required to take.[15] After this scandal, McLaughlin left the Assembly, although he has been allowed to salvage his political career. As I write these words he is a county executive.

Two years earlier, a similar incident occurred in the New York State Assembly: Assemblywoman Angela Wozniak had a sexual relationship with her male director of legislation. When he broke up with her, she proceeded to harass him and gave him poor performance reviews. Like McLaughlin, Wozniak was publicly sanctioned. In her case, the ethics committee also called for an independent investigator to conduct a climate survey of all of her employees.[16] After this scandal Wozniak did not seek reelection.

In both cases, the New York State Assembly exemplifies what organizations can do: go beyond the letter of the law to stop sexual misconduct as soon as it occurs and contain the damage, with an eye toward changing bad behavior rather than destroying careers. Even if some forms of misconduct—lewd jokes or intimate hugs, for example—aren't quite illegal, they might still be unethical, toxic for team morale, and bad for business. Compliance with the law may be enough to avoid lawsuits, but on its own compliance usually is not enough to create a workplace free from harassment, retaliation, and the associated damage to organizations when they fail to retain key talent.

In the next two chapters I'll look at how individuals and

organizations can play a role in developing workplace cultures that promote inclusion and that allow employees to flourish and thrive—whatever their background or identity. Many standout players are holding themselves to higher standards than the law requires. And, as we'll see, they are reaping enormous rewards as a result.

8

INDIVIDUAL ACTION STEPS

As an individual in a large organization, here's what you *can't* do: change the corporate culture to make professional relationships safer and more trusted. That's a long-term task for the organization, which we'll examine in chapter 9. But individuals *can* take action and make a difference. Some measures can have a positive effect right away and are appropriate for both junior and senior employees to take. Others are longer term and help pump up the prospects for true inclusion in leadership. These will reduce the locker-room mentality and skewed power relationships that have made so much sexual misconduct possible. For these latter, more transformative measures, managers and executives will need to take the lead. In this chapter, we'll take a look at both: the small action steps individuals can take today, and the big ones that will help create a better tomorrow.

SWEAT THE SMALL STUFF: STEPS TO PROTECT YOURSELF AND THOSE AROUND YOU

1. Don't Touch or Otherwise Invade Personal Space

It's surely not good for a politician when the top Internet search linked to his name is "creepy." Yet that's the situation in which former Vice President Joe Biden found himself in the spring of 2019. As the *New York Times* pointed out, Biden is an "old-school backslapper" whose "tendency to lavish his affections on women and girls was so central to his persona that it became fodder for late-night television jokes."[1] However, a number of women have made clear that they didn't find the joke funny: his habit of touching and hugging and pulling them close, or even kissing their necks or heads without permission, made them deeply uncomfortable.

Biden and many women and men who know him well have described his physical affection as benign, affectionate, or avuncular; several have noted that when he was a young man such behavior was entirely normal. That is all surely true, but one of the attitudinal shifts that #MeToo is helping lead is that women now insist on the right to decide how others treat their bodies. It isn't for Joe Biden or his friends to say whether or not it's appropriate for him to plant a long slow kiss on a young woman's head. It's for the woman to say.

In the workplace, everyone should respect each other's personal space. (If you want to be precise, anthropologists estimate that anything closer than eighteen inches is invasive, unless you're close friends or family.[2]) In an interview, Sharon Ryan notes that International Paper (IP) is a company that values relationships and fosters a culture in which people care and watch out for one another, with many coworkers forming valuable friendships on the job. Close relationships shared by friends and team members are sometimes reflected in pats on the back and sometimes even hugs in the workplace, but that doesn't change the rule that we need to be respectful of one another's personal space. "Bear hugs aren't for everyone, especially at work. We encourage sensitivity to how any form of touch might be perceived. It's also important to be mindful of cultural differences in greeting styles. The preferred business greeting in the United States is a handshake, or for those we know well, a one-handed side hug. But don't be offended if a colleague from another country greets you with a kiss."

Men, too, will appreciate respect for their personal space. Steven Imrie, a lawyer who also happens to be a powerlifter with more than fifty championship medals to his name, has a physique that attracts attention. One day, when he was at his job as a legal counsel at a *Fortune* 500 company, a high-ranking woman walked up and squeezed his biceps. (Imrie was conservatively dressed for casual Friday, in a short-sleeved polo shirt, though he nonetheless asked himself if he had somehow dressed too provocatively.) "We had a cordial professional relationship, but we didn't know each other well," he recalls. "Immediately I thought, *Well, this is interesting. What if I turned around and squeezed your breasts?* I would have been in big trouble if I'd tried to return the 'compliment.'" If you respect others' personal space, and politely insist that they respect yours, you will be helping to make your workplace safer and more comfortable for everyone.

2. Don't Dress Provocatively or Otherwise Signal Sexual Availability

Sharon Ryan, general counsel at International Paper, joined the firm in 1988, just a few years out of law school. At IP itself, she was always treated with respect; however, she sometimes encountered harassment at trade shows, where older men would try to take advantage of young women there to represent their companies. But such men didn't expect to meet a woman like Ryan. "If any guys crossed the line, I'd just tell them in no uncertain terms to go away and stay away," she recalls. "I've always been tough, but as a result of those trade shows, I learned to be more intentional about maintaining a strictly professional demeanor."

Today, she is fierce in her advice to women . . . and men. "I tell them, at company events, do not overdrink, maintain your professionalism, and call it a night at a reasonable hour. And look like a professional at all times. I particularly caution women to be responsible with their clothing and to dress for respect. There have been times that I have asked women to go home to change. How you dress for private social functions or on your personal time is your business, but dressing provocatively at work or work events is never appropriate."

It may sound harsh—and certainly, innapropriate clothing is never justification for harassment or assault—but any woman or man should primarily be on the job to do the job, and clothing and behavior should reflect a commitment to career and profession.

It's not just junior people who would do well to heed Ryan's advice. When Erin Callan became CFO of Lehman Brothers in 2008, shortly before the firm collapsed, she posed for a series of photos for a Condé Nast magazine, *Portfolio*. One showed her in a very low-cut top. Another showed her in a short skirt, displaying long legs as she stepped out of a limousine. *Fortune* reported on her "ever more provocative wardrobe," noting that "her skirts were short and her tops tight."[3] *New York Times* columnist Andrew Ross Sorkin's book remarked on her "Sex-in-the-City style stilettos."[4] *Fortune* (among others) called her the "Greta Garbo of Wall Street."[5]

I don't know if Callan suffered sexual harassment at work. I hope that she did not, and if she did, it was certainly unjustified, no matter how she dressed. But Callan did not help herself by her self-presentation. If supervisors, coworkers, and clients are discussing a woman's cleavage, or how a man looks in his tank top on a casual (but surely not *that* casual) Friday, they are probably not also discussing that person's professional accomplishments. Many will perceive "come hither" accessories as an invitation to treat that person as no more than a sex object. As I discussed in my 2014 book, *Executive Presence*, dressing provocatively is the number-one mistake for high-performing women on the fast track—it undermines a woman's "gravitas" and knocks her off the list of serious contenders for an executive position.[6]

The reality is, whether you are junior or senior, man or woman, you should relentlessly telegraph professionalism at work. That means both how you dress and your wider, personal brand. How you decorate your office and cubicle, for example, will tell your supervisors and coworkers a lot about your priorities. So will the ways in which you talk about your romantic life.

Professionalism need not mean dressing like a nun. You absolutely can be chic—even elegant. But you should not present yourself in a way that distracts or causes discomfort and misunderstanding. A professional "client ready" look won't just reduce the chances of unwanted sexual advances or malicious gossip, it will *increase* the chances of other men and women feeling comfortable hiring or sponsoring you, being hired or sponsored by you, or simply working with you. It will also make workplace friendships—based on respect and trust—easier to form.

3. Don't Meet in Bars, Hotel Rooms, or Apartments

Who likes to meet subordinates in hotel rooms? Famously, Harvey Weinstein had a habit of inviting young women to meet him for "business meetings" at his hotel room, where he greeted them in his bathrobe, then groped or raped them. Weinstein wasn't the only one. In an earlier chapter, I mentioned briefly the ongoing $30 million lawsuit brought by Sara Tirschwell, a senior executive at a Wall Street asset manager. Tirschwell accuses her boss of having pressured her into sex and she accuses her company of firing her when she complained.

According to her lawsuit, at the last moment, her boss—the alleged assailant—changed a meeting from a restaurant in a hotel lobby to his apartment in the same building. Tirschwell claims that he opened the door of his apartment dressed in a bathrobe, and as he invited her in made clear that he "expected sex as part of their business meeting."[7] Her boss denies any sexual relationship with Tirschwell, but he admits that they on several occasions held one-on-one meetings in his apartment.[8]

I do not know what happened or how a court will rule. But I would guess that holding one-on-one meetings with Tirschwell in his apartment, when so many other locales were available, at the very least weakens his defense—both in court and in the opinion of his colleagues and the board of directors of his company.

There's a better way, one that keeps everyone both safe and above suspicion: meet in an office with an open door, or a local coffee shop, or any other setting that lends itself to transparency. Mark Hanson, a senior vice president at Freddie Mac, told me where he deepens relationships with protégés, male and female. "The company cafeteria," he says. "That's where we meet as I seek to understand a little bit better about where they're coming from and what they're seeing. People don't interrupt and the phone isn't there. Breakfast, lunch, even just coffee, it's all good."

If you and a colleague are traveling together on business, don't hold your late-night prep for the next morning's presentation in your hotel room or a bar. Have it in a safe zone: the hotel lobby, or one of the conference rooms or business centers that every major hotel has. If you're the senior person, just set the prep meeting up that way. If you're the junior person, suggest, and if necessary, politely insist on meeting in a safe zone. The cost of renting a conference room is a small price to pay for avoiding malicious gossip—and, perhaps, genuine discomfort on your colleague's part.

To avoid favoritism, you will need to avoid late night one-on-one meetings in hotel rooms and bars with *both* genders: you cannot stay up late at a corner table with John, but not with Joan, or vice versa.

4. Don't Flirt or Sleep with Someone Very Junior to You, Very Senior to You, or Married to Someone Else

The data in chapter 2 shows clearly that when office affairs cross lines of hierarchy the whole workplace environment becomes toxic. An earlier CTI study found that 84 percent of men and 93 percent of women disapprove of affairs between managers and subordinates.[9] The impact of workplace relationships is far reaching. Kevin Lord, now head of Human Resources at Fox Corporation, remembers well an early experience in his career when his coworker was having a relationship with their boss.

"I can tell you firsthand that a workplace relationship can greatly impact the entire team," he says. "Early in my career, I worked for a company where the head of HR, whom I was reporting to, was having an affair with a peer. At the time of the affair, my boss was married and my peer was not, so the relationship was under wraps and there was a lot of subterfuge. It affected all of us. We had to deal with secrecy, favoritism, and preferential treatment. Their relationship severely impacted employee morale and trust—we all became hesitant to discuss work issues with our peers because it would immediately get back to our boss, oftentimes 'out of context.' If you feel that the playing field isn't level, it's disheartening."

Lord's story exemplifies how illicit affairs can harm team dynamics, especially when a supervisor is involved: the boss is no longer seen as fair-minded and favoritism is now thought to affect assessment and promotion processes. A common result is disengagement and flight risk. Now, in his capacity as head of HR, Lord supports and implements policies that address inapropriate supervisor and employee relationships in the workplace.

Oftentimes the more junior partner in an illicit affair (or romance) is also damaged. For every Tina Brown who marries the big boss and kick-starts a spectacular career and a lasting marriage, many more young women and men find themselves used and abused. Maya Lanier,* a marketer at a luxury appliance firm, told me about a colleague whom I'll call Elaine, who did her best to flirt her way to the top. "She would wear form-fitting blouses, and in meetings she did that kind of sparkly-eyed flirting thing with the boss, Ben," Maya recalls. "She'd touch his shoulder or touch his hand and make some joke that was slightly racy but could be perceived one way or another, you know, the double entendre thing." Ben took the bait, says Maya. "He started giving Elaine the best work. He listened to her advice. They often went out for long lunches. Everyone assumed that they were having an affair.

"But Ben was married, and she ended up meeting someone else and dating him. Her boyfriend was very overt about his love; he'd send her flowers at the office. It was in Ben's face, and suddenly he started trying to humiliate her, treated everything she said as stupid. Elaine happened to be very talented, and she knew it. She realized things were going badly wrong, became agitated, had a big blowup with Ben, and quit." Maya found the whole scenario infuriating, in part because she saw Elaine as a talented woman who had squandered her professional capital. "I really wanted to tell her: your skills are super impressive, you don't have to do this."

---

* Name changed at interviewee's request.

5. Don't Be Tardy, Defensive, or Self-Absorbed— and If You Need to, Say Sorry and Mean It

"Social norms have begun to change, they've shifted, and the boundaries of protecting personal space have been reset and I get it. I get it. I hear what they're saying." That was what Joe Biden said, in a video on April 3, 2019, some five days after women had started to come forward to complain about what they considered inappropriate touching. During those five days, he had issued three statements, through spokespeople. This video was the first attempt to speak on the subject himself—and it left some people dissatisfied. For one thing, it was five days late. For another, the video didn't contain an actual apology. "Imagine all the time he could have saved," one woman wrote, "by typing 'I'm sorry. I will do better.'"[10]

But perhaps the most tone-deaf attempt at remorse came from a man who—unlike Joe Biden—appears to have been a repeat sexual predator: more than twenty women have accused Jian Ghomeshi, a former broadcaster at the Canadian Broadcasting Corporation (CBC) of acts of sexual abuse, which include biting and choking. The courts have acquitted him of some charges and he's settled others, but in his September 2018 essay, "Reflections from a Hashtag," he was full of pity—for himself. "There was a sentiment among [my accusers] that, regardless of any legal exoneration," he wrote, "I was almost certainly a world-class prick, probably a sexual bully, and that I needed to be held to account beyond simply losing my career and reputation." He added, "I cannot just move to another town and reboot with a pseudonym. I'm constantly competing with a villainous version of myself online."

Further down, he does admit, briefly, that "I ought to have been more respectful and responsive with the women in my life. To them I say, you deserved much better from me."[11] That was the closest he came to an apology, before he resumed lamenting his lost career and friends, wallowing in resentment, proclaiming that he learned from his mistakes, and generally displaying a dizzying sense of entitlement. If Ghomeshi intended to kick-start his rehabilitation, he failed spectacularly: the essay provoked outrage. It even cost the editor who had published this piece his job.

Other predators have issued similar non-apologies. Harvey Weinstein, for example, attributed his actions to having come of age in the sixties and seventies, "when all the rules about behavior and workplaces were different." I happen to remember the sixties and seventies quite well: rape was against the rules then, too. Matt Lauer issued an apology that at least was an apology: "There are no words to express my sorrow and regret for the pain I have caused others by words and actions. To the people I have hurt, I am truly sorry. . . . The last two days have forced me to take a very hard look at my own troubling flaws. It's been humbling. I am blessed to be surrounded by the people I love. I thank them for their patience and grace." Fine words, but it is hard to avoid the sense that a crisis management firm wrote this statement for him. After all, Lauer fought the accusations bitterly until the evidence became overwhelming. It also seems strange that he needed "a very hard look" to understand that sexual assault is wrong.

How *can* sexual predators apologize effectively? Danya Ruttenberg, a prominent rabbi, offers some advice. "Repentance is really hard work, in contrast to the glib and easy way these accused perpetrators are seeking cheap forgiveness from popular culture," she wrote in the *Washington Post* in September 2018, adding that the most critical factor, repentance, or *tshuvah*, requires that "the bad actors must own the harm perpetrated, ideally publicly. Then they must do the hard internal work to become the kind of person who does not harm in this way—which is a massive undertaking, demanding tremendous introspection and confrontation of unpleasant aspects of the self. Then they must make restitution for harm done, in whatever way that might be possible. Then—and only then—they must apologize sincerely to the victim. Finally, the next time they are confronted with the opportunity to commit a similar misdeed, they must make a different, better choice." Ruttenberg suggests a few ways to demonstrate good faith on the path to forgiveness: "A shift in priorities, an investment of their wealth or time into work protecting victims of assault and harassment or creating policies that would better prevent abuse."[12]

6. Be an Upstander—Not Just a Bystander

If you witness a blatant case of sexual harassment or assault at work, you should speak up, at the moment, if possible. Then go to HR and let the victim know that you'll serve as a witness if needed. But besides the scenario of clear-cut sexual misconduct, there is another all-too-common scenario in many workplaces: witnessing an incident that isn't blatant misconduct—and is probably not illegal—but it makes everyone uncomfortable. Maybe it's a male colleague who hasn't groped or made a pass at anyone but constantly comments on the clothing and attractiveness of the young women who work for him. Or maybe it's a female colleague who likes to crack dirty jokes and weaves sexual innuendo into every conversation.

For those who find these comments and jokes offensive, it can feel like death by a thousand cuts. Yet most members of the team might respect this person's work, or find him/her a good colleague overall, even if they would like to cut out the creepy commentary.

In this situation a formal complaint might not be helpful, as HR and legal departments aren't equipped to handle complaints about behavior that is demeaning but not illegal.

Here is where bystanders can become *upstanders*: men and women who catch and call out microaggressions and disrespectful behavior. If you're a manager or supervisor and the creep is on your team, have a word with him or her. If you're a coworker or a direct report, seek an ally: a manager or executive higher in the hierarchy who would be willing to speak to him or her. Naturally, it will be far easier for bystanders to become upstanders if the corporate culture supports them—but that is a topic that I'll address in chapter 10, as a part of a deeper look at organizational action steps. First, let's look at more things that individuals can do, not just to have an immediate impact but to help sow the seeds for longer-term, organization-wide change.

SEIZE THE BIG STUFF: USE SPONSORSHIP (SAFELY!) TO BE A TRANSFORMATIONAL LEADER

As discussed in chapter 7, in the era of #MeToo, a lot of good men are running scared and heading for the hills, diluting or abandoning advocacy efforts for female protégés. CTI data shows that nearly two out of five women agree that "recent publicity about sexual harassment at work makes it even less likely that a male leader will sponsor a female protégé—no matter how high performing she is, even if she deserves it," while Pew found that 55 percent of men say that the focus on sexual harassment and assault has made it harder to know how to interact with women in the workplace.[13]

That's a tragedy, and not just in the moment for the women and men concerned. Sponsorship is critical to female progression, as senior-level advocacy is essential for anyone wanting to rise up the ranks into leadership. It is also true that creating a culture of inclusive sponsorship is critical to the bottom line, as diversity around decision-making tables is a competitive edge in an increasingly multifarious and multipronged marketplace. McKinsey, for example, recently found that companies with a significant number of women on their executive committees had a 47 percent greater return on equity and 55 percent higher operating results than companies with no women at the top.[14]

Just as important, in the era of #MeToo, diverse leadership helps right the power imbalances that have made sexual harassment and assault so common. As explored in chapter 3, women can be predators just as men can be, and it would be foolish to say that if a company has more women at the top, sexual misconduct will automatically stop—but it will be ameliorated.

I've spent the greater part of my career advising organizations on diversity and inclusion, and it's clear that a diverse executive pool supports a respectful, inclusive culture. When organizations work to level the playing field so that more women, people of color, and LGBTQ individuals can rise on their merits, then they are also creating a workplace environment that isn't about alpha-primate dominance games. Such workplaces make it easier for everyone to speak up, whether it's to offer an innovative idea or to condemn harassment and assault.

To create such a workplace, those who currently hold the power will need to sponsor more women and individuals from diverse backgrounds, compensating for their lack of an old boys' network, and giving them the same leg up that young white men from the right schools and backgrounds have always had. But in the era of

#MeToo, this kind of sponsorship requires a new approach, both to keep participants safe and to be truly effective. Here are five tips to make sponsorship—whether of young women or young men— a lever for positive change for you, your protégé, and the organization you work for.

Be Public

If you're a senior manager meeting with a prospective protégé who does not look like you, and you are thinking of giving him/her a big opportunity, don't do it behind closed doors. Do it in public and make sure everyone sees what you are doing and why. It's not just a matter of avoiding misunderstandings, it's a matter of *creating* understanding. You're well advised to put that junior person in front of colleagues, so they, too, can see their value and why you're advocating for him or her.

In 2016, Tiger Tyagarajan, CEO of professional services giant Genpact, brought in a much younger, attractive young woman, Katie Stein, to be the firm's new chief strategy officer. Stein had a superlative résumé—a track record of success at Boston Consulting Group—but few people read each other's résumés before meetings. In a technology-focused company such as Genpact, where men dominate the top ranks, women, especially young, attractive ones, attract scrutiny and skepticism.

Three months after hiring Stein, Tyagarajan put her in the most public position possible: he assigned her the pivotal task of presenting the company's strategic plan at its annual investors' day, in front of Genpact's board of directors and most important investors. She hit it out of the ballpark. After her presentation, there was no room to question her role at the company or what the CEO had seen in her—it was obvious to everyone that it was her ability, not her good looks. As Tyagarajan recalls it, "After she spoke, one of our biggest investors came up to me and said, 'Where'd you find her? She was great!' He was closely followed by my chairman, who said, 'She did a fabulous job.'" When a top shareholder and the chairman of the board spontaneously compliment your hire, you can rest assured that no one is whispering behind your back.

Not everyone is in a position to put a high potential young talent in front of the board of directors. But if a junior person you're advocating for has great ideas or particularly strong credentials in a field the company needs, make sure to share this information with colleagues and put him/her in front of them. Encourage your protégé to make presentations to internal stakeholders, although—as any good leader does with up-and-coming talent, of either gender—you will likely want to work with them first.

Before that pivotal investors' day, Tyagarajan had worked with Stein to refine the company strategy and had given her advice on how to handle different stakeholders. In other words, Tyagarajan set Stein up for success, treating her as he would any other superbly talented colleague he'd recruited for the firm. He was just especially careful to do all of this *in public*. Tyagarajan knew that if his advocacy of Stein was 100 percent in the open, it would leave gossips nothing to mutter about.

Be Noisy

This piece of advice is an extension of *be public*: don't just be transparent. Actively and loudly broadcast what a relationship is doing for you and the company. When Michael Roth took over as chairman and CEO of advertising giant Interpublic Group (IPG) in 2005, he found that the company had a big problem. "It was all white males at the top," he says. "That's crazy for an ad company. From a business point of view, we have to pay attention to what the world is like." At the time, IPG had a chief diversity officer, a charismatic and impressive African American woman named Heide Gardner. But she was, Roth says, "window dressing and everyone knew it."

Roth met with Gardner, heard her ideas, and decided that she was the one to help IPG develop a workforce that could better reach and serve a global marketplace. But he also realized that he needed to protect both himself and Gardner from charges of favoritism. Roth solved for this by calling a meeting with the heads of IPG's various brands and divisions—and brought Gardner in to formally "reintroduce" her. "I told them," he recalls, "that diversity was going to be part of our DNA and that I was going to take immediate steps to make that happen. In particular I was going to make them accountable, and Heide would be in charge. 'She'll work with you,' I said, and 'she'll have programs,' but she'll report to me directly, and when Heide says, 'We need to do this or that,' think of it as me telling you, 'You need to do this.'"

There's no room for anybody to suspect back channels or illicit relationships if the CEO calls a meeting and says, "This person has a *direct* channel to me, and her agenda is a top priority for me because its central to the health of our company going forward."

Just as important—especially in a company with little history of women and diverse talent at the top—broadcasting Gardner's value helped Roth establish an inclusive leadership culture: one in which women and people of color are there not as decoration or to meet a quota, but because they have a job to do and the company values that job. Such an environment helps all employees feel safe, that they belong, and that they have the same opportunities as anyone else—because they do.

Be Humble

When Subha Barry was a managing director at Merrill Lynch, in charge of multicultural business development for wealth management, her job was to help Merrill reach and serve diverse communities. She did so very profitably, with tailored services for her own South Asian community, as well as for African Americans, Hispanics, and women. Seeing her success, a young associate named Todd Sears came to her with an idea for marketing wealth management services to the LGBTQ community.

Barry loved the idea, and she was humble enough to let *him* take the lead. "Just as I had great familiarity with the South Asian community," she recalls, "he had a very personal knowledge of the LGBTQ community, knowledge that would have taken us a lot of research and money to replicate." Barry was respectful and didn't try to tell him what to do—but she didn't give him a blank check either. "I gave him fifteen thousand dollars and said, 'Use this and show us what you can produce on your own. I need proof of concept. If you can pull off a win, I can then persuade the company to invest big and go national.'"

Barry's approach—giving Sears a small budget and specific goals, then standing back to see if he could deliver on his promises—simultaneously empowered Sears and put both of them above reproach. It also created an impressive stream of value. "Within a year, year and a half, he brought in the assets," Barry says. "The multiplier was quite tremendous. I don't remember how much his business grew at the start, but I have to tell you, the order of magnitude was tremendous. He took that fifteen thousand I gave him and he showed us that if we invested in his community, there was enormous business to be done." Barry then persuaded Merrill Lynch to bankroll Sears so that he could go national and train financial advisors at offices around the country to serve the LGBTQ community. Sears eventually created a business worth $1.4 billion to Merrill and he's always given Barry a great deal of credit.

Barry was an incredibly effective sponsor of Todd Sears at least in part because she was humble—and open—about what she didn't know and respectful of what he could bring to the table. As a result she was able to partner with an openly gay LGBTQ activist in a conservative organization and together they were able to build a $1 billion-plus business.

Share Life Experiences—but Don't Overshare

Bonds of camaraderie and trust can and should grow in the workplace, and there's no reason they can't cross demarcation lines of race and generation as well as gender and sexual orientation. You can open up, be vulnerable, and invite a colleague of a different identity to be vulnerable, too—but only if you can do it in ways that aren't threatening or sexual, and don't provide grist for salacious gossip or sneak attacks on social media.

Kevin Lord, who heads up HR at Fox Corporation—we met him earlier in this chapter—has built a valuable relationship with the Diversity & Inclusion Leader, Marsheila Hayes, an African American woman. This relationship began not at Fox, but at another media giant, Gannett, where Lord was also head of HR and Hayes was a Talent Acquisition Manager. At that time Hayes had just graduated college and was many levels in seniority below him. They met through a "reverse mentorship" program at Gannett, which partnered senior managers with high-potential junior recruits, so that millennials could tutor baby boomers on, for example, digital skills. (As I'll discuss in chapter 9, programs that formalize professional interactions across generational and other divides are excellent corporate action steps in the era of #MeToo.)

Hayes gave Lord valuable insight on how to use social media

and how to benefit from new digital platforms, and her guidance was concrete and practical. Lord learned to appreciate her skill sets and her work ethic. He considered how he could mentor her with a goal of becoming her advocate, and championing her. Recognizing he was a senior executive, he also thought of a way to engage her in a more casual setting where they could have a conversation more as coworkers. So, over coffee in the company cafeteria, he asked her for some advice. Lord's son—a junior in college at the time—was exploring various career paths and had turned to his dad for help. "What should he do to make himself more marketable?" Lord asked Hayes. "Are there career fairs you recommend he attend? Internships he should consider?" As Lord remembers, Hayes "had lots of good recommendations. She later told me that she was thrilled that I asked for her advice. It made her feel that I was treating her with respect—like a peer."

After having been invited into Lord's world, Hayes was ready to share hers. She asked him for advice on whether she should go back to graduate school, and if so, where. He told her he thought she should analyze the costs and the benefits of attending different graduate schools. Indeed, Lord went to the trouble of putting together a cost-benefit analysis to help Hayes make the decision. Hayes was immensely grateful—graduate school was a financial stretch for her (she intended to do it part-time while holding down a full-time job), so she appreciated Lord's help in making a wise investment decision.

This two-way stream of advice cemented their professional relationship. "We've listened to the things that matter to each other," Hayes says, "and found ways in which we could contribute value to one another . . . we built trust."

In early 2017 Lord accepted a position at Fox News as head of HR and committed to lead an effort to transform the workplace culture after the ousting of Roger Ailes and in the wake of lawsuits over sexual harassment and racial discrimination. Lord knew he could not do it all on his own. He knew that he needed to build a diverse team that he could trust.

So Lord did the obvious thing: he picked up the phone, called Hayes, and offered her an opportunity to join his team. "When he called me up and told me about the opportunity at Fox," Hayes recalls, "my response was that I didn't know very much about Fox. But I took the job, because I trusted him as a leader. I still do."

Be Boisterous about the Benefits

A generation or two ago, there was a widely shared reason behind why employees were suspicious about a close relationship between a senior man and a junior woman: many simply did not accept that a woman *could be* a top professional performer. Many assumed that the boss had to be sleeping with the young woman he was spending so much time with, because they could not imagine any other motive for him to be with her. Even now, especially in male-dominated professions, some men are skeptical of women who receive fast promotions. Perhaps they're sleeping their way to the top? Or perhaps the company wants to check a box on a diversity checklist to please a few social impact investors?

The antidote is for senior men to talk up what is a proven fact: diversity (as in gender, ethnicity, sexual orientation, and other dimensions of difference) boosts the top and bottom line, with improvements in innovation and new market growth translating into higher revenue and profits.[15] The entire workforce—not to mention the board of directors—should understand that giving women and people of color a fair shot at opportunities is both just *and* good for the company. With that understanding in place, when older men give talented young women what they have always given talented young men—attention, guidance, and encouragement—others are more likely to understand that such relationships are a business imperative.

Consider Steve Howe, the recently retired US chairman and Americas managing partner at professional services giant EY. Howe did not simply sign his name to the firm's various programs that have boosted the presence of women, LGBTQ employees, and other diverse individuals in the senior ranks. He personally publicized these efforts, through magazine interviews,[16] blog posts,[17] company-wide memos,[18] interviews,[19] and through chairing the firm's Inclusiveness Advisory Council.

Even more important, Howe has personally sponsored many promising women and men and encouraged his protégés to sponsor other protégés, thus triggering a "cascade" that has transformed leadership at the firm. In 2018 the board voted to make one of his protégés, Kelly Grier, his successor as US chair and managing partner. "For the first time," Howe told me shortly after the board's vote to name Grier, "EY will have a woman at the helm, but Kelly is not there because she is a woman. She is there because she was the best candidate for the job."

Top-performing women in leadership and in senior management make it easier for men and women to work together, support each other, and sponsor each other with full transparency and trust—and that is helping EY and firms like it avoid the costly hits to the talent pipeline that (as described in chapter 6) so many companies are unnecessarily suffering from.

In the era of #MeToo, everyone, man or woman, senior or junior, can take steps to make the workplace environment safer and more respectful. In the next chapter we'll look at what companies can do—and in some cases are already doing—to drive more enduring change.

9

COMPANY ACTION STEPS

#MeToo took companies unawares. In the words of one Wall Street titan I interviewed, "There definitely was a 'deer caught in the headlights' moment, but we've rallied and many of us have tightened our game."

As we will see in this chapter, this "tightening of the game" has been noteworthy, and it is ongoing and even accelerating. This is clear not only from the news headlines (such as those cited in chapter 1) but also from the interviews I did in early 2019 with leaders such as Citi's Bradford Hu, IBM's Diane Gherson, International Paper's Sharon Ryan, and Freddie Mac's Ricardo Anzaldua. They all believe that the #MeToo movement, and the need for companies to respond to the pain and damage it has brought to light, is far from over. Across a range of industries, from Microsoft and Google to IPG and Fox News, companies are experimenting with new ways of preventing sexual misconduct. Many business leaders are responding to the pressure points—particularly those "hits to the bottom line" described in chapter 6—but some are plunging in with a commitment that goes way beyond financial self-interest.

Michael Roth, CEO of advertising giant IPG—we met him in chapter 8—has taken on a tough challenge: transforming a leadership culture in an industry that is riddled with out-of-control male "stars" and hushed-up scandals. As #MeToo has gained steam, so has the outrage at all-too-quiet dismissals often accompanied by payouts and soft landings. Starting in the fall of 2017 insiders in the advertising industry began naming and shaming sexual predators on Instagram in an account called "Diet Madison Avenue."

Roth's response was bold. He sent an e-mail blast to IPG's fifty thousand–plus employees promising a "zero-tolerance policy for all types of harassment at IPG" and urging anyone who suffered or witnessed such behavior to report it to management, human resources, or the legal department, without fear of reprisal, or to report it anonymously through the IPG alert line.[1]

Even as employees were reading the memo, a test was in the works. Apparently unbeknownst to Roth, an IPG affiliate, the Martin Agency, was investigating its chief creative officer, Joe Alexander, over several decades' worth of allegations of sexual harassment. Alexander, who was behind Geico's gecko and other hit campaigns, was fired in December 2017 and left the old-fashioned way: quietly, with no acknowledgment or apology.[2]

But the news leaked out. Stories spread about Alexander and the misogynist *Mad Men* culture at the Martin Agency. Amid growing outrage, six days after Alexander's firing, the Martin Agency's CEO, Matt Williams, revealed more details about the misconduct and admitted to a "painful wakeup call." Roth saw the need for more than a wakeup call. He replaced Williams with Kristen Cavallo—the agency's first female CEO—amid a leadership shakeup that soon included the appointment of a chief cultural officer. Cavallo has spoken freely about #MeToo accusations in local media interviews and encouraged accusers to come forward. In one interview she talked about her admiration for those who speak up, saying, "Do you know how hard it must be to break something you love in order to make it better?"[3]

With the new year came a new test: Nancy Mucciarone, a former employee, claimed in a lawsuit that another IPG agency, IPG Initiative, failed to act after she reported a client for pulling her shirt open and groping her breast. While the client company had immediately fired the man in question, Mucciarone's supervisor at IPG Initiative had waited several days before even reporting the incident. Roth's zero-tolerance policy kicked into gear and IPG Initiative's CEO, Amy Armstrong, did *not* try to sweep sexual assault under the rug. She sent an e-mail to the entire staff explaining what had happened, emphasizing that employees should immediately report inappropriate behavior, and encouraging them to go directly to her if necessary.

Zero-tolerance policies are not for the fainthearted (see the section on "legal backlash" on page 16), but when a CEO not only sends an e-mail but also follows through, installing a new female leader at one troubled affiliate and fully supporting another to turn things around at another affiliate, change takes hold. It's particularly gratifying to see such change in advertising, an industry with particularly high rates of sexual harassment and assault. CTI data (see chapter 2) shows that across media and advertising, a startling 41 percent of women and 22 percent of men have experienced sexual harassment at work.

"There's a particular sense of entitlement in these cultures," says Heide Gardner, chief diversity officer at IPG. "Creative people in creative environments like to think that they're different and need to be insulated from the kind of structure and process you might find in other industries. There's a belief that in the ideation phase rules can be broken—nothing is sacred. We like to see ourselves as a kind of an un-profession in terms of not being buttoned-down. But we're getting more buttoned-down when it comes to codes of conduct that prevent sexual misconduct."

What exactly does "buttoned-down" mean when fighting sexual

harassment and assault? Based on the data and the interviews I've marshaled for this book and my many years of experience helping corporations build inclusive cultures, I've identified five action steps for organizational change. The first two steps are already spreading. Steps three and four are more of a struggle, but some companies are partway there. Step five, which holds the greatest potential, is still "aspirational" for most organizations. But I'm optimistic. With so much at stake, forward-thinking companies will surely get there.

STEP ONE: TAKE A STAND

Update Core Corporate Values

Values aren't platitudes. If a company stands behind them and rewards them, they matter. Charles Galunic, a professor of organizational behavior at INSEAD in Paris, says that corporate values are always a "wish list." Yet a study he helped lead nonetheless found that when companies actively seek to shape their culture, they outperform peers—especially if they keep adapting these values. "In effect, 'tweaking' their values shows that these companies are actively trying to reform and improve themselves, which we believe is connected to their financial performance," Galunic wrote. "A wrestling match with your culture can be a valuable exercise and is the real value behind espousing corporate values."[4]

That's why Uber, which has been plagued by allegations of misconduct (see chapter 6), is, under Dara Khosrowshahi's stewardship, working to make respect and inclusivity a key part of a culture that is both competitive and leaves no room for sexual harassment or assault. The original Uber values that featured "stepping on toes" and "principled confrontation" have been thrown out. Instead, Khosrowshahi has installed eight new, inclusive values that include "we celebrate differences" and "we do the right thing."[5]

Establish Zero Tolerance

Every employee, from the CEO to the stockroom clerk, should know that credible evidence of sexual misconduct is grounds for immediate termination—without a lucrative severance package and an innocuous press release that claims that he/she is leaving for personal reasons. A sexual predator should not get rewarded with a comfortable and honorable early retirement. Contracts may make it hard to avoid granting predators golden parachutes, but it's possible.

Les Moonves's contract with CBS, for example, promised him $120 million in severance unless he was terminated for "cause." "Cause" for termination can tricky to prove. In Moonves's contract, violations of company policy only counted as cause if they produced a "material adverse effect." In such cases, many companies simply prefer to make the payout and move on, but CBS took a stand: its board connected the revelation of Moonves's pattern of sexual harassment and assault to a hit to the share price (a "material adverse effect") and refused to pay him. University of Oregon law professor Elizabeth Tippett notes that the stock market impact was, from the point of view of justice, a lucky break. "Had the reports been less public, or Moonves less famous, it would have been a much harder case to make," she says.

Tippett therefore argues (and I agree) that contracts must define "cause" far more strictly, especially for the most senior executives: many executive agreements contain loopholes that require policy violations to be "willful" or "material," while for less senior employees, any violation of policy is grounds for dismissal.[6] Zero tolerance means that everyone should be held to the same standards, ones that absolutely and explicitly forbid harassing or assaulting colleagues—and zero tolerance should also extend to retaliation over complaints. "We have a very straight-forward policy over retaliation," Diane Gherson, chief human resource officer at IBM, told me. "It's a fireable offense."

Place the CEO Front and Center

For a zero-tolerance policy to work, the CEO has to demonstrate, in words and actions, that this is the stand he or she is personally taking. That's why, as described earlier, IPG CEO Michael Roth sent out an e-mail to every employee—and why he stepped in to change the leadership at an affiliate that had failed to act appropriately against a sexual predator.

It's also why Abigail Johnson, chairman and CEO of Fidelity Investments—the firm her grandfather founded—recognized that when a sexual harassment crisis hit in 2017, she had to shake up the old boys' club. Under her watch, the firm dismissed two top portfolio managers in response to credible allegations of sexual misconduct at work. She then sent out a questionnaire, discovered that most women and people of color felt out of place at Fidelity, and took action. She physically moved her desk onto the floor where the portfolio managers sat. The symbolism was powerful—in this open-plan situation she could literally keep a closer eye on the department that had been so troubled by sexual harassment. She also redoubled the firm's efforts to diversify leadership and required unconscious bias training for all employees.[7]

Salesforce CEO Marc Benioff is another leader front and center in these battles. He's focused on closing the pay gap between men and women in his company and has emphasized that equal opportunities, equal advancement, equal pay, and zero tolerance for sexual harassment all go together. He makes this policy clear in his everyday actions and by shouting those actions from the rooftops. To take just one example: "I am not going to have any more meetings," Benioff said on national TV, "that aren't at least a third women."[8]

Move from Compliance to Proactive Measures

At Uber, Susan Fowler had all the evidence in the world to prove sexual harassment: screenshots of her manager's messages about his search for new sex partners, as well as corroboration from other women at the firm—and still, at first, HR didn't act. (Only later was the manager let go.) It's the problem with a culture that only looks at compliance: unless a case rises to the level of a felony, no one may act, and senior management may never even hear of the alleged transgression. Top executives and board members, who see their focus as narrowly defined business issues, might not even choose to be looped in to such matters. Although these decision makers are *supposed* to meet risks head-on, in practice, many at the top suffer from FOFO: Fear of Finding Out. However, especially in the #MeToo era, sooner or later the public *will* find out, with likely a big impact on the company brand and its valuation.

Top executives must instead invest in a culture of respect, rewarding those who denounce misconduct and encouraging everyone to "sweat the small stuff" before predatory behavior becomes a big business risk. To paraphrase the management guru Peter Drucker, "culture eats compliance for breakfast" and then you move on to the big stuff at subsequent meals. Fernanda Beraldi, senior director of ethics and compliance at Cummins, has been leading an initiative that encourages a strong culture of respect. Among the tools that Cummins uses to foster such a culture in the #MeToo era are senior-level focus groups, with invitations sent out by the CEO, that focus on training leaders to both avoid and deal with sexual harassment and involve skilled facilitators from HR, legal, and compliance. Beraldi also finds and enlists people the company calls "champions" to answer colleagues' questions about what to do and where to turn if they suffer or witness misconduct of any type.

When it comes to sexual misconduct, IBM has developed its own very high standards. For all 380,000 IBM-ers this standard lays out what the company considers sexual harassment and assault, as well as conduct offenses, such as bullying. "We are a global company and we have global standards," says CHRO Diane Gherson. "If someone violates our standards, even if they do not violate the law of the country where they work, we will take appropriate action."

To develop these standards, Gherson went on a global listening tour, gathering employees' experiences and studying local cultures and regulations. Among her surprising discoveries: the legal protections against sexual misconduct vary dramatically, and traditional western, industrialized cultures don't necessarily have the stongest protections. Gherson's active efforts to seek out different perspectives—and value what she gleans—is a wonderful example of inclusive leadership.

Global Connections and Connectors

How do you enlist people to lead cultural change in a business that spans two hundred countries? Fernanda Beraldi at Cummins believes Malcolm Gladwell offers an answer in his book *The Tipping Point: How Little Things Can Make a Big Difference* with his concept of "connectors": people who know how to galvanize others and spark word-of-mouth epidemics.

Connector/champion isn't a job title. Where such people fit

in the hierarchy doesn't really matter. "It's those people who are natural leaders," says Beraldi. "Every organization has them and knows who they are. So why not enlist connectors to talk to their colleagues about the ideal corporate culture? Ask if they're willing to be facilitators of focus groups. When they travel on business, are they willing to meet with people in the places they go and talk about what an ethical culture means? They can also lead the way in pointing out when someone allegedly exhibits bad behavior. They shouldn't be the ones to report it, but they might be available to colleagues who have questions about what to do and where to turn."

STEP TWO: TRAIN AND COACH DIFFERENTLY

Turn Bystanders into Upstanders

"If one person speaks up when something happens, there's a contagious effect. If you see something inappropriate and act on it, that disrupts the culture of silence." So says Asha Santos, an employment lawyer who has developed "bystander intervention programs" for several companies, including Unilever, JetBlue, Edelman, and Skadden Arps. Individuals must speak up to support victims and denounce sexual predators, but doing so takes courage and involves personal risks—unless the organization takes steps to make upstanding easier than bystanding.

Such steps should start at the top, Santos says, with a message from the CEO that bystanders must speak up, with no fear of retaliation. Santos also suggests putting managers and staff together in bystanding training seminars, to make clear that misconduct and its denunciation have no hierarchy—the responsibility is collective. Training seminars should explore (either through videos or playacting) common scenarios of misconduct in the workplace and involve participants in a discussion about how to respond.

For example, in workshops Santos sometimes shows a video in which actors depict executives, two men and one woman, at a business dinner with a male client. The client starts hitting on the woman by putting his hand on her arm. Each of her male colleagues responds—which is good—but their responses are inadequate. One texts her and says, "I see what's going on and I'll understand if you want to leave."

"That," explains Santos to the workshop participants, "is telling her that they don't actually need her at the table." The other male colleague asks, "Are you doing okay?" "That's an opener," Santos says, "but it still doesn't shut the behavior down."

She then asks workshop participants how the bystanders could do better. "I hear a lot of suggestions," she says. "Some say the men should be confrontational, others that they shut the client down with humor. The second suggestion might work because the goal here is to shut down the behavior quickly and lightly. If the aggressor persists, one of the men should pull the client aside and tell him he can't do this."

One result of "upstander" training is a happier and more productive office environment. As discussed in previous chapters, witnessing bad behavior has a toxic effect not unlike secondhand smoke, especially among men. CTI data shows (see chapter 2) that 45 percent of men and 52 percent of women who had witnessed some form of sexual misconduct were dissatisfied with their jobs.

At IBM, Diane Gherson has found a "great appetite" for programs that turn bystanders into upstanders. "People are only too willing to speak up," she says, "they just need a little training on how to say something in the moment to diffuse the situation. It can be as simple as saying, 'Hey, could you repeat that?' Oftentimes, the other person will then say, 'Whoa, I didn't intend for it to come out like that. I apologize.'"

One video IBM uses as part of its upstander training shows a junior employee named "Carrie" and her manager "Lance." Lance asks Carrie to stay late to help finish some reports. Carrie, who had noted Lance's interest in her work and assumed it was a testament to her skills, agreed. Reports done, Lance tries to kiss Carrie, who pushes him away. "Bad career move," Lance says—but another employee named "Frank" happens to pass by and see the attempted kiss. Frank, astutely and appropriately, makes his presence known and Lance leaves in a hurry. But now Carrie is fearful of losing her job in retaliation. What should she do? How about Frank? Is it any business of his, now that Lance has left?

The video then gives viewers multiple options, eventually recommending that both Carrie and Frank report Lance immediately, using one of the many channels that IBM offers, without any fear of retaliation, since Lance's behavior violates IBM's policies—though if Carrie wishes to handle the matter on her own, she has that choice and can tell Frank so.

Create a Speak-Up Culture: If You See Something, Say Something

It's hard for bystanders to speak up, but it's even harder for the victims to do so. As we saw in earlier chapters, victims fear indifference, shame, ridicule, or retaliation—and those fears, alas, are all too often justified. It's possible to change that. International

Paper's general counsel, Sharon Ryan, explains how. "It's about actualizing respect and making sure that there is no retaliation for speaking up, and that everyone knows that," she says. That means publicizing that the company has a speak-up culture, with the board of directors backing it up. It means a robust help line. It means swift action when misconduct is uncovered, no matter the tenure or position of the perpetrator. "I'm shocked at how flat-footed some companies have been," she says. "Leaders and boards act as though the organization would fall apart if one particular top executive were pushed out. But the tone at the top matters enormously, and no one is indispensable. You just can't protect your leaders if they have done something bad on this front."

Every report of sexual harassment should be investigated, and if the report involves a senior manager, the company should bring in an outside investigator as an affirmation of the company's commitment to fair, objective judgement. Companies should also work to make senior management more diverse. "Let's face it," Ryan says, "until you have a significant number of women in leadership, the teamwork among leaders to do the right thing for everyone doesn't have the well-rounded perspective it needs to be totally effective could." Generally speaking, people at any level of an organization can have skeletons in their closets and may cover up for one another, undermining a culture of transparency and respect, but the damage is especially demoralizing when leaders are involved. To help support a speak-up culture, Ryan wants all of a company's senior management to understand what's at stake. "Our brand in this space really makes a difference to our ability to attract and retain great people," she says. "At IP, our employees, men and women, shouldn't have to worry they're going to open the pages of the *Wall Street Journal* and read some scandalous story about our company, so we take steps to protect our culture and integrity."

Create and Celebrate Men as Allies

Men should not feel threatened by #MeToo. They should feel empowered. One reason is that (as chapter 4 described) a significant minority of men are victims, too, and #MeToo offers these men greater safety and dignity. #MeToo also offers men the chance to collaborate with women and with other men in richer, more productive ways. After all, if you're a man seeking to rise, you'll want to find friends and allies in the entire talent pool, not just those who look like you. As the sociologist David Smith says, "Being a good mentor or ally to people expands your network across the organization and even externally. More diversity in your network gives you access to more information. All of that gives you influence." A study by Smith and the psychologist W. Brad Johnson found that "white men are not penalized for publicly valuing diversity . . . Although men may fear reprisal for championing diversity and inclusion initiatives, or feel it's not their place, the evidence is clear that they have little to lose."[9] In other words, advocating for women is all gain and no risk.

But there's a right way and a wrong way to go about it, and Smith and Johnson run exercises to teach men the right way. In one, women form an inner circle, with men forming an outer circle around them. Only the women are allowed to talk, describing an average day on the job. "Men's eyes get wide," says Johnson. "You can see that they're kind of stunned—later they might say they had no idea how it feels to be a woman in a male-dominated environment." Then the men move into the inner circle and talk while the women listen. Finally men and women brainstorm together on how to handle sexual harassment or sexist comments. In another exercise, men and women role-play and get feedback from the audience, with the goal of making both men and women more confident in working with and supporting each other.

In one such exercise, a man playing the role of a manager offering advice to a junior female colleague simply blurted out, "I'd like to mentor you." Audience members often squirm. "Datey," a participant said in one seminar. "Mentor you" might sound like a euphemism for a less printable verb. "So that leads to how you have a conversation that isn't loaded with other baggage," says Johnson. "The man could say, 'I saw your presentation in a meeting, and I was impressed. I see you as a rising star, so feel free to drop by anytime if I can be of help.' That sort of invitation leaves it up to her. It feels more transparent."

IBM is actively cultivating allies through its Be Equal program that invites male and female employees to pledge specific actions (around awareness, respect, and accountability) in recorded videos, with the goal of fostering workplaces that welcome men, women, people of color, LGBTQ individuals, and other potentially targeted groups.

In a moment of reflection at the end of our interview Gherson stressed the importance of a "road to rehabilitation" for some sexual harassment offenders, potentially turning them into allies. "If misconduct is repeated or egregious, there is no room for the offender in our company," she says. "But if it's the first offense, and relatively mild, we have a conversation. We look to see whether they're repentant, understand their mistake, are empathetic with the victim, and are willing to commit to training. In some cases it's just a matter of failing to understand what is acceptable in today's workplace. Many folks are able to redeem themselves."

When I heard about IBM's road to rehabilitation I could not help but think about the troubling case of former US senator Al Franken. In the fall of 2018 Franken was accused of sexual misconduct, denied due process, and forced to resign his Senate seat by fellow senators intent on other agendas. As a well-researched piece by Jane Mayer in the *New Yorker* lays bare, these career-ending actions hinged on a flimsy charge leveled by a right-wing media personality who had her own fish to fry.[10] As Mayer points out (and I think Gherson would agree with her) when we treat all allegations in the same way, it feeds into a damaging backlash narrative: men are vulnerable to even frivolous allegations by women. Due process and proportionality of response are critical if #MeToo is to enhance the lives of women.

Better Training and the Road to Redemption: A Conversation with Carol Goodman

Carol Goodman, a partner in the New York law firm Herrick, Feinstein LLP, is a specialist in sexual misconduct law. These days she is mostly helping client companies train staff, from board members to executives to line-level employees, on how to change the corporate culture to prevent sexual misconduct from ever occurring. At Twenty-First Century Fox, for example, she has trained thousands of the company's employees.

In sessions, Goodman gathers a roomful of employees from every level of the hierarchy—this encourages a back-and-forth discussion of how coworkers can treat one another better. "At the beginning," she says, "I was thinking of having separate sessions for managers and staff. It turned out that by hearing different perspectives, employees got more out of the session." For the staff members, she says, being in a training session with executives of the company conveys a sense that those at the top care. "If you're sitting in a training session next to an executive of the company, you get the message that the company is serious about this and that no one, not even a top executive, is excused from training."

Unsurprisingly, Goodman has found that creating trust in an organization system is a process. In order to convince employees that it is safe to report sexual misconduct, she has to make sure the company sends a clear message that retaliation is prohibited.

In her training she explains to managers, with specific examples, what is and what is not retaliation because it is not always obvious. That's why part of Goodman's training highlights that retaliation will result in disciplinary measures. Such safeguards against retaliation are critical, Goodman says, because once an investigation begins, the accuser will be informed of the complaint and the identity of the accuser.

She also warns employees in her sessions that after a complaint is made, social pleasantries between the inidividuals are probably going to break down. "If your boss no longer pops his or her head in and asks, 'How are the kids?' that is not retaliation," Goodman notes. "But the company's senior management must ensure that aside from abandoning social interactions, it's business as usual. For example, the boss cannot cut the employee's bonus or pay, or give a poor evaluation, or remove the employee from an assignment because an employee has filed a complaint. I have had to guide managers through that process because the first action is commonly: 'This employee complained about me and I want them fired.' I explain to the client that we're going to have to figure out a different way forward."

"At many training sessions, supervisors have asked, 'Who protects me? Someone can just falsely accuse me, how am I protected?' Retaliation does not come into play if an employee falsely accuses a supervisor. A complaint must be made in good faith. So, the answer is that investigations must be thorough. Investigators need to speak with every person involved," she explains. "You talk to witnesses to help put the facts together. You look at e-mails and texts and anything that is relevant."

Some people ask why there should be any problem if a sexual encounter is consensual. Goodman says that an older senior executive asked her that question. Her response was, "If you are the boss, you will never really know if your employee is consenting or just protecting themselves. If a senior powerful executive, such as yourself, is asking out a twenty-three-year-old intern, odds are, she is afraid to say no because she wants to keep her job."

With discussions as concrete and hard-hitting as these, Goodman sees rigorous training as a road to understanding and—possibly—redemption. It certainly provides answers for the powerful executives who claim they're afraid that one misplaced compliment or joke will destroy their career.

"Corrective action should depend upon the severity of the situation." One type of corrective action Goodman discusses is a mandatory 'one-on-one training program'—at the employee's own expense. Underwriting the cost of the training might not be outlandishly punitive for a well-paid executive, but even so, it has a psychological impact."

"Of course, I'm not talking about repeated or egregious offenses," says Goodman, "but in cases where the offenses are minor, losing a bonus or having to pay for a private training program sends a strong message to the offender. In a one-on-one training I can also focus on specifics: what they've done and what they could have done differently. I have been involved in situations where this works—where the offender remains in their job, and the conduct does not reoccur."

Goodman's accomplishments are remarkable, but while many of her real-life examples involve men as the aggressors and women as the victims, chapters 2 through 5 of this book show that sexual misconduct comes in other forms, too.

Teach about Toxic Masculinity

The vast majority of men are not sexual predators. But nearly every man has been among other men who belittle women, gay men, or anyone else who's not "one of the guys." Such men display toxic masculinity, which unfortunately is common. "I grew up in the cult of masculinity," Terry Crews (whom we met in chapter 5) wrote. "What it came from is literally a belief that as a man you are more valuable than a woman. The reason I have the authority to say this is because I was like that. I truly believed I was more valuable than my wife and kids."

If a man, however decently he treats women in his own life, keeps silent around this kind of toxic talk, he is aiding and abetting it. Yet it is so pervasive that, as Blaine Townsend, a senior vice president at the ethical investment firm Bailard Wealth Management, puts it, "Toxic masculinity is something you don't perceive as a man until a woman points it out to you."

Many men do indeed need guidance on how to identify and stop toxic behavior, but the good news here is that other men (and women) are stepping up to the plate to provide it. The male-led NGO A Call to Men, for example, conducts seminars for corporations and sports teams. "The world is going through a paradigm shift that men don't know how to navigate," says one of its founders, Ted Bunch. "We're used to blaming women for what men do." An African American, Bunch remembers women in the civil rights movement telling men about oppression within their own ranks. "The women were supposed to take the notes, cook us meals, and otherwise stay out of the way," he recalls. "They had to come forward—we wouldn't have recognized it on our own."

In training sessions, Bunch and his partner Tony Porter present a diagram, "The Man Box," which outlines society's expectations for men: powerful, fearless, emotionless, dominating, and success-ful, whether in the boardroom or the bedroom. They then help men question these expectations and encourage participants to start changing the behavior toward women that such expectations have led to. "When you combine male privilege with financial power or other kinds of power, it can be a dangerous thing," says Bunch. "Our message to men is that we need to be responsible with our privilege—and that we gain from bringing equality to others."

STEP THREE: UPGRADE REPORTING, RESPONSE SYSTEMS, AND DATA COLLECTION

Create Multiple Reporting Systems (Including One That Is Anonymous and One Direct to the Board)

If an employee reports sexual harassment or assault, many HR departments' top priority has been to avoid a lawsuit—and avoid the need to fire or reassign the "brilliant jerks" (high-performing executives) who have been accused. In these circumstances HR often would ignore—or even hide—incriminating evidence. This attitude is changing, as awareness grows that sexual misconduct is a business risk, but not every HR officer has gotten the message, and as a result, many employees do not trust HR to protect them. That's why companies must offer more than one channel to report misconduct. Asha Santos recommends that every employee should have a list of at least five people who they can contact if necessary, as well as a telephone hotline.

IBM, for example, has a safe line called Talk It Over. Diane Gherson explains, "It's a confidential line, which allows employees to brainstorm as well as report a specific incident. It could be, 'Hey, I have a situation I want to discuss. I'm not sure I want to report it. I don't even know if what happened qualifies as bullying or harassment.' Once the discussion happens, the HR professional on the other end may say, 'To take this forward, I'm going to need to use names, but here's how I'll use them. Here's who will know.'" Gherson notes that, to protect innocent individuals, IBM does not permit anonymous accusations, but the company wants to encourage those who truly did suffer misconduct to come forward for advice.

Should creating an in-house hotline be impractical, several third-party providers offer web-based hotline services that enable employees to report harassment, as well as other kinds of misconduct.

Companies should also offer boards of directors direct and speedy access to allegations of sexual misconduct. Even if a supervisor or someone in HR is able to resolve the problem, the top brass should know what's happening at every level of the organization because of the threat sexual harassment and assault poses to the bottom line. Boards of directors expect to be quickly and completely informed if an executive—or a division—has put the company at risk by selling a defective or unsafe product (just think of Boeing). Sexual misconduct falls into the same category because, like safety violations, it can trigger a hit to company brand and a huge drain of value. Companies should therefore ensure that boards of directors have direct access to reports of misconduct.

Incentivize Reporting

Here's an idea that may seem counterintuitive, but it works: reward managers who increase the number of reported incidents of sexual harassment and assault. The reality is, higher rates of reporting signal a success story—at least in the short run. They mean that a manager has succeeded in creating a trust-filled workplace that has encouraged both victims and witnesses to report. In the long run the number of reported incidents will drop as the team learns how to be more inclusive and respectful and more and more bystanders turn into upstanders.

Another tip aimed at managers: take care to track developments *after* a complaint is lodged, and make sure that accusers know what steps are being taken. "If someone reports a case of sexual harassment or other policy violations, the person charged with investigating the matter should get back to them as quickly and frequently as possible," says Fernanda Beraldi.

Use Information Escrows to Enable Confidentiality

At Uber, Susan Fowler eventually discovered from colleagues that her manager was a serial predator; HR had records of other complaints, including from senior executives, but kept them secret. Secrecy is not the way to go. Companies—and their risk officers and boards—need to know if multiple complaints are piling up against a single employee. However, if supervisors or HR handle each complaint discreetly and in isolation, they can effectively bury this information.

One solution is an "information escrow," which allows victims' complaints to be collected in a database. All complainants are anonymous, but a complaint is reported to senior management if two or more employees lodge a complaint against the same individual. The idea is to allow anonymous accusations—which may be all that some victims are comfortable with—but at the same time, build in an alert that warns a company if complaints are mounting up against a potential "bad apple."[11] Several such information escrows are already in the market. Callisto, for example, was developed as a tool for reporting sexual assaults on college campuses, but now has a platform for companies, too. Others, such as Warble and Pluto (see sidebar below), allow employees to report other problems besides sexual harassment.

Pluto's Information Escrow: How Martin Fogelman Hopes to Change the World

Pluto is a start-up platform that allows employees to report sexual misconduct and discrimination anonymously, then stores the details in an information escrow so that top executives at a company can be alerted if a big problem is emerging. Martin Fogelman, Pluto's CEO and founder, says data on misbehavior in the workplace can do more than just expose offenders. "This kind of data should be seen as a risk-management tool," he says. "Sexual harassment isn't just a compliance issue; it is a mainstream business issue."

Fogelman launched Pluto in 2016, when he was just twenty-six. His original intent was to collect data on all kinds of social impact. "But," he says, "we began to see that D&I [diversity and inclusion] was the area where companies most needed metrics, and inclusion is the metric that's most correlated with business performance."

After the #MeToo movement started to make headlines, Fogelman saw his fledgling database as a tool that could build transparency about sexual misconduct as well as provide greater depth on D&I. "The two track and are inseparable," he says. "Sexual harassment happens most often in workplaces that are dominated by a homogenous group," Fogelman says. "Almost always the dominant group is white cis-gender men. And here is the nub of the problem: the more privileged a person is—the more catered to—the less likely that person is able to understand the problems that come with exclusion. Privilege to the privileged becomes invisible. It's like air. So sexual misconduct is oftentimes invisible to men at the top, and compelling data— especially when it describes risk—can make the invisible visible."

As with other information escrows, client companies make Pluto's platform available to their employees. Anyone who feels that he/she has experienced sexual misconduct, discrimination, or microaggressions can report it anonymously through Pluto's online database. The employee has a choice and can file an informal complaint describing the incident or a formal complaint describing the incident and naming the aggressor. If (and only if) other people in the organization also file complaints about the same aggressor does an alert go out, and it goes out to both those who reported the incidents and to those with authority to take action. Such multiple complaints are frequent, Fogelman says. "Statistically, if someone acts in an abusive, aggressive way, they're likely to do it time and time again."

The company can also use Pluto to ask every employee to describe—anonymously—how they perceive the work environment. This data can be cut by gender, ethnic background, and sexual orientation and serve as a barometer for bias and bullying.

Naturally Pluto's platform is effective only if the company uses it well. Fogelman tells potential clients that Pluto won't do much if the only people who see complaints are compliance or

HR officers. Top executives must overcome their Fear of Finding Out, since sexual misconduct and exclusion can impact business outcomes. "Boards of directors should be in the loop," says Fogelman, "because what if several employees report the CEO as a sexual predator?"

Upgrade Data Collection

The data presented in chapter 2 shows what is happening in companies across the face of the US economy, broken down by industrial sector. But what's happening in your company? What are the legal and reputational risks that you potentially face from sexual scandals? Are you already taking a hit in recruiting, retaining, and engaging talent because of misconduct throughout the ranks? Could you soon face an exodus of top executives as Nike did? How many of EEOC's top risk factors (see sidebar on page 37) do you face? Beyond the risks, are you seizing talent acquisition opportunities—by making women, people of color, and LGBTQ individuals see your company as an employer of choice and by making them eager to offer new ideas?

There's only one way to know: measure and map inside your company the way CTI's survey measured and mapped across sectors and industries. Figure out who's at risk, what the risks are, and where they are greatest; discover patterns of misconduct, who and what does and doesn't get reported, and how bystanders react. Get leadership the data it needs and update annually to measure progress. Such data can also help develop an inclusive leadership culture (see below), which not only fights sexual misconduct but also boosts innovation and financial results.

"There's been a tipping point," says Pooja Jain-Link, executive vice president and head of research at CTI. "In-house legal counsel and HR are starting to realize that they need to know what's going on when it comes to sexual misconduct. In the past they were concerned about legal liability, about what the company knew, but it's getting to the point where not knowing is a greater liability than knowing. You don't want to risk finding out from a newspaper headline or from social media. Find out first from your own survey data and take appropriate preemptive action." Jain-Link adds that, "It's particularly helpful to ask employees if they've reported all instances of sexual misconduct they've either experienced or witnessed, so that you know what percentage of incidents are making their way into the system—and to have an open response section in the survey for respondents to explain why they did or didn't report."

As Mark Twain famously put it, "It ain't what you don't know that gets you into trouble. It's what you know for sure that just ain't so." Make sure that your company isn't in that situation.

STEP FOUR: OWN YOUR PAST

Create and Share an Honest Narrative About the Past

I spoke in chapter 8 about the importance of individuals acknowledging past bad behavior. The same is true for organizations. Victims will not speak up and bystanders will not become upstanders unless they're firmly convinced that the organization takes sexual assault and harassment seriously. Men and women throughout the ranks will not feel motivated or empowered to come forward and take action unless they see their organization take responsibility for past misdeeds.

A few months after #MeToo burst into the headlines, NPR's popular broadcast *On the Media*, which scrutinizes media behavior and ethics, had an unusual target: itself.[12] John Hockenberry, it turns out, a longtime talk show host at WNYC (an affiliate of NPR, which produces *On the Media*), had been credibly accused of forcibly kissing at least one woman on his staff, groping and harassing others, and bullying several female cohosts. He was quietly dismissed by WNYC, but there was no publicity about the accusations against him, until various news outlets broke the story.

Now *On the Media* played clips of its own coverage of this incident, including a news show where Brian Lehrer grilled WNYC CEO Laura Walker on why Hockenberry's misdeeds had been covered up. Walker apologized, but also said there was much she couldn't talk about (including Hockenberry's severance package) because it was "a confidential personnel matter." Lehrer challenged that confidentiality. "Is it the right policy?" he asked. "What I can tell you is that it's a policy we are revisiting," Walker responded. It was a frustrating response.

Clearly, the culture at WNYC has been and is imperfect, but reporters aren't shying away from presenting an honest narrative. (To offer another positive example, CBS News has reported on its own board investigating Moonves and covered the demonstration outside its annual shareholders' meeting after Moonves's firing in 2018.)

Walker, who mentioned during the Lehrer interview that she had been sexually harassed herself (without giving specifics), has since stepped down, issuing a statement to staff saying she and the board "have agreed that the time has come for me to move on." WNYC has also fired hosts Leonard Lopate and Jonathan Schwartz after surfacing credible sexual harassment allegations against them. Kudos go to WNYC for finally publicizing these incidents and its own flaws in covering them. This is what the struggle to create and share an honest narrative looks like.

A radio station has a natural channel to publicize its narrative, but other companies can find ways of doing this, too. The faster the company goes public, the more control it will have over the narrative in the face of 24/7 news cycles and social media posts. As mentioned in chapter 1, when news of sexual misconduct at Deloitte UK emerged, its CEO, David Sproul, didn't just fire the offenders, he released data describing the problem. Which underscores another benefit of creating an honest narrative—Sproul's transparency obliged Deloitte UK's competitors to follow suit: PwC's, EY's, and KPMG's UK operations have all, subsequently, taken similar measures. The *Financial Times* has urged them on: "As vast laboratories of white-collar work, the Big Four ought to be leading the way in rooting out and preventing bullying and harassment, and setting an example to companies in other sectors, many of which are their clients."[13] At least in the United Kingdom, accounting firms have started to take that lead.

Get the Mea Culpa Right

Beyond offering transparency about the past, organizations must also apologize to victims. This can kick-start a change in the corporate culture. But to achieve this goal, an apology must be more than a statement of general regret for unspecified harm and a vague promise to do better. For guidance on what a real apology looks like, let's return to the advice of Danya Ruttenberg, a much respected rabbi who was quoted in chapter 8: "The bad actor must own the harm perpetrated, ideally publicly. Then the bad actor must do the hard internal work to become the kind of person who does not harm in this way again—which is a massive undertaking, demanding tremendous introspection and confrontation of unpleasant aspects of the self. Then they must make restitution for harm done, in whatever way that might be possible."

Own the harm. Do the work. Make restitution. These are all hard steps, with legal counsel potentially warning leadership of risks for each. But, as chapter 6 shows, the risk of continuing to sweep misconduct under the rug is greater still, while (as I will discuss in a moment) getting inclusion right can massively strengthen both the corporate culture and the bottom line.

Let's consider this in the light of scandals within the oldest continuously functioning institution in the world: the Catholic Church. For decades, as most of us now know, the Church harbored predatory priests who sexually abused boys and young men—and at least some girls and women. The Church responded by protecting . . . the predators. It covered up the incidents and transferred predator priests to other parishes, where they often continued to abuse children.[14] It took far too long, but finally, in August 2018, Pope Francis apologized: "It is essential that we, as a Church, be able to acknowledge and condemn, with sorrow and shame, the atrocities perpetrated by consecrated persons, clerics, and all those entrusted with the mission of watching over and caring for those most vulnerable. . . . We showed no care for the little ones; we abandoned them. . . . The extent and the gravity of all that has happened requires coming to grips with this reality in a comprehensive and communal way. While it is important and necessary on every journey of conversion to acknowledge the truth of what has happened, in itself this is not enough. . . . We have delayed in applying these actions and sanctions that are so necessary, yet I am confident that they will help to guarantee a greater culture of care in the present and future."

Own the harm. Do the work. Make restitution. The Pope is here doing the first, explicitly and publicly, and promising the second and the third. It's a good start, and other parts of the Church have started to do the work and make restitution—beyond what lawsuits have already obliged. The United States Conference of Catholic Bishops, for example, has removed a cardinal and former archbishop from the ministry, started a full investigation into his misdeeds, approved a third-party reporting system, and begun work (in consultation with parents and outside experts) on a code of conduct.[15]

Oregon State University is another organization that finally seems to have issued a satisfying mea culpa—after a woman contacted both the university and a journalist to reopen the story of her 1998 gang rape by OSU football players. Though the university and the police had not apologized for the incident when it happened, this time around, OSU president Edward Ray conducted an investigation, issued a moving apology letter, then hired the victim, Brenda Tracy, to a two-year position at the university as a sexual violence consultant.[16]

Own the harm. Do the work. Make restitution. That's what a real mea culpa looks like.

STEP FIVE: EMBED INCLUSIVE LEADERSHIP BEHAVIORS

A report by CTI, "Innovation, Diversity, and Market Growth," pinpointed six key behaviors that make for inclusive leadership: seeking out and valuing different perspectives; showing informed empathy; encouraging and enabling risk-taking; giving actionable feedback; conferring authority; and sharing credit.[17] These six behaviors, the study showed, help create workplaces that enable men and women to work together in harmony, speak up freely, and advance according to their merits. That kind of workplace leads not just to a reduction in legal, financial, reputational, and talent retention risks in the #MeToo era, it also provides benefits for innovation and new market growth. CTI data shows that employees (whether male or female) on teams with inclusive leaders are more likely, compared to employees on teams without inclusive leaders, to feel:

- welcome and included (87 percent vs 51 percent)
- free to express views and opinions (87 percent vs 46 percent)
- confident that their ideas are not only heard but valued (74 percent vs 37 percent)[18]

If you feel welcome, and if you feel free to speak up, confident that your ideas will be listened to and respected, then you are clearly working on a team where sexual misconduct is rare. You are also likely working on a team where innovative ideas bubble up, with men and women of every background eager to contribute to productivity and growth.

Inclusive leadership, by making everyone welcome, helps keep talent of all kinds engaged at work and rising through the pipeline. That creates diversity in top jobs around decision-making tables, which is critical both to fighting sexual misconduct and to achieving marketplace success. CTI data shows, for example, that employees in publicly traded companies with diversity in leadership (gender, race, and sexual orientation, among other forms of difference) are far more likely to report improved market share (48 percent, compared to only 33 percent of companies without diverse leadership) and capturing a new market (46 percent vs 27 percent) over the previous twelve months.[19] It's common sense, really: if you have a diverse group of leaders and a diverse workforce that feels safe, respected, and empowered to innovate, then that company is more likely to succeed in an increasingly multifarious and global marketplace.

In other words, by fostering inclusive leadership, companies have an opportunity to meet the challenges of #MeToo and boost the bottom line at the same time. This idea is not utopian: many companies already are doing it.

UK banking giant Barclays, for example, took an idea from the co-chair of its employees-with-disabilities affinity group and created a nationwide system of ATMs equipped for visually impaired customers. That both grew Barclays's market and boosted its brand. Cisco's multibillion dollar smart grid initiative began with an executive training program that consciously sought out top talent that crossed lines of difference—particularly the divides of generation and gender—and taught participants inclusive leadership skills. Silicon Valley law firm Fenwick & West leaned on its women's network to create a flexible employment model that has enabled the firm to employ more attorneys from nontraditional backgrounds—and grow its client base. Standard Chartered Bank's first-ever female head of branch banking in India reached out to professional women to find out their specific and differentiated needs and created two branches staffed entirely by women. These branches broke records, becoming the most profitable in the region.

These are just a few examples of how inclusive, diverse leadership does not just prevent bullying and harassment, it also unlocks innovation and boosts new market growth in very concrete ways. All that, combined with the growing "drain of value" associated with sexual misconduct, should be leading every company to strive to be more inclusive.

White Male Entitlement vs Women's Issues in the Presidential Race

Beto O'Rourke, who at this writing was one of the twenty-five Democrats vying to be the presidential nominee in the 2020 election, began to fall out of favor, at least with the media, after a *Vanity Fair* profile quoted him saying, "I'm just born to be in it." He later apologized in an appearance on *The View* but, as *Vanity Fair* put it in a followup story: "that single quote read to many as an emblem of white male privilege in a Democratic primary that was already pulsing with identity politics."[20]

Meanwhile, other candidates have been talking about issues of importance to those less certain of their privilege. Senator Kamala Harris of California, for example, came out with a proposal to proactively close the gender pay gap, which has been an almost surefire way to keep workplace power in the hands of men. Under Harris's plan, instead of the onus falling on employees to report or sue their companies if they suspect sex discrimination in salaries, companies with at least one hundred employees would have to certify that men and women are paid equally.

Throughout this book, I have argued that sexual misconduct at work is all about power: a person with outsize authority weaponizes sex to strengthen or reassert their dominance over "others." The big shots with outsize authority are generally (but not always) older white men in senior positions. The targeted group is often (but not always) younger women in junior positions. As we have seen, women with outsize authority can also be predators, and men, particularly gay men and men of color, can also be prey.

Fundamentally, the "others" are outsiders who threaten to di-lute the perks and privileges of a charmed inner circle we often call the old boys' club. Harassment and assault have been a way to let outsiders and interlopers know that, no matter how talented or valuable, they will never be fully welcome inside the club.

Power and its perks are addictive, and many who have power now will fight tooth and nail to keep it. Many will fight even though a more level playing field would benefit their companies. Sally Krawcheck, CEO of Ellevest and former president of Global Wealth Management at Bank of America, told me, "It doesn't make sense to have the top of corporate career ladders comprise a wall of white men. There are a ton of bottom-line reasons why there should be many more women and people of color in the C-suite." But, she adds, "I've learned that economic logic doesn't always win."

How can we make economic logic, as well as simple justice, win? The legal, structural, and cultural changes I've discussed in this book are aimed, ultimately, at breaking up the old boys' clubs (and the occasional old girls' club, too) to create a more diverse and inclusive workplace culture. This shift is a radical one, since it requires more than a token woman or person of color at the top. It is no coincidence that the EEOC places "a homogenous work-force" at the top of its list of risk factors for sexual harassment (see page 37). When workforces are homogenous, those who are different are more likely to be isolated and vulnerable. Those in the majority, meanwhile, often feel empowered to threaten indi-viduals who are different and will seek to "put them in their place" through various tools, including sexual harassment and assault.[21]

If merely a handful of diverse individuals are promoted into executive ranks, and workplaces remain overwhelmingly white, male, and heterosexual, with the same values and culture as before—

then the few women, people of color, and LGBTQ individuals who do rise to the top may mimic the old boys' club. They may weaponize sex, bully, and harass their own subordinates as they too seek to dominate and establish authority. It is therefore essential to have a critical mass of diverse talent at the top, as well as a deep, diverse bench and talent pipeline.

Truly diverse leadership tends, as the data shows, to be inclusive leadership, which creates a welcoming environment for all employees, as well as a speak-up culture that fights misconduct and supports innovation. Inclusive leaders view sexual dominance games at work as counterproductive, since sexual harassment and assault harms, hurts, and excludes individuals who could bring ideas and energy to the table and seed organizational renewal and growth.

The economist Herbert Stein famously said, "If something can't go on forever, it will stop." #MeToo has shown that the time has finally come to stop sexual misconduct and to build workplace cultures where everyone has the power to speak up and be heard. It is my hope that this book helps make the case for inclusive cultures and provided guidance for how to make them a reality in organizations around the country, starting now.

AFTERWORD

As this book goes to press, the #MeToo movement continues to ripple and roil through our workplaces, liberating victims, wounding power brokers, dividing constituents, and driving—at least some—societal change.

In late August 2019, the legendary tenor Placido Domingo became the latest superstar to have his reputation tarnished—if not ruined—when eight female opera singers and one dancer came forward and accused him of sexual misconduct. The allegations span decades, with accusers saying Domingo used his position as general director at the Los Angeles Opera to offer women career advancement in exchange for sex. They also allege that he "punished" women who rebuffed him—taking their names off audition lists and refusing to write recommendations.

The Domingo case has split the opera world. While the San Francisco Opera and the Philadelphia Orchestra immediately cancelled engagements with Domingo, several European organizations decided to go ahead with planned appearances. Indeed, Domingo received a standing ovation when he performed at the Salzburg Festival on August 25—the first time he had walked out onto a stage since the scandal broke.

The Domingo case drives home where we are today: a world that is struggling to both believe the victims *and* embrace due process. The latter means not only holding accused perpetrators innocent until proven guilty but also scrutinizing the severity of the offense so that punishment can be proportionate. These new dilemmas thread through this book, and while I want to pay tribute to the difficulty of the challenges faced, the very existence of such dilemmas shows how much headway the #MeToo movement has made. The fact that divas such as Patricia Wulf as well as graduate students such as Nimrod Reitman are able to give voice to their pain—with the expectation that they will be heard and something will be done—is a huge step forward.

Two weeks after the Domingo case hit the headlines, a searing exposé on sexual abuse of men in the US military was front page news. On September 9, the *New York Times* ran a poignant piece that lifted up the voices of six victims: men like Jack Williams, assaulted in boot camp by his drill sergeant, who choked him until he passed out then raped him over a desk. The sergeant's final words to him were "If you report this, no one will believe you." And he was right; until recently, no one would have.

Ten thousand men are sexually assaulted in the American military each year. In the past, only 3 percent reported. As we know from chapter 4, male victims have been too humiliated to talk and male leaders, in the military and elsewhere, have been in chest-thumping denial ("real men" would not allow this to happen). Since #MeToo, rates of reporting among male victims in the military have surged—according to some research, as much as five-fold.

The #MeToo movement scored one other clear win this last summer. On August 14, New York joined several other states in enacting a Child Victims Act (CVA). Previously, victims of child sexual abuse in New York had to file charges by the time they were twenty-three, but the new law extends the statute of limitations to the age of fifty-five. Victims can now file charges against a child sex offender as well as the organization that let it happen—for several decades after the abuse took place. This expanded "look back" law is much needed. Child abuse victims are often very young when they are harassed or assaulted—five, ten, twelve years old—and the abuse often takes many years for these youngsters to process what they've gone through. In the past when they were ready to file charges, they often found that they had no recourse because of state limits on the time they had to file. That is now changed. In the days after Governor Andrew Cuomo signed the bill, accusers came forward with complaints against an astounding array of organizations: the Governing Body of the Jehovah's Witnesses, the Archdiocese of New York, the Boy Scouts, the New York City Department of Education, and Rockefeller University in Manhattan. There is now a fighting chance that these august bodies will be held accountable.

In chapter 7, I show how legal remedies to these problems of sexual harassment and assault were very slow to get off the ground. But our legislators and our laws are now gearing up and contributing enormously to the cumulative momentum of #MeToo. They're set to reinforce the significant efforts of "better angels" in the corporate community to help guarantee enduring change.

AUTHOR'S NOTE

All information about ongoing matters mentioned in the book are up to date as of August 2019.

ACKNOWLEDGMENTS

I have found researching and writing about #MeToo an extraordinary experience. Fast-evolving and full of wrenching pockets of pain as well as glimmerings of hope and action, this movement is critically important to our nation. For years to come our values, our culture—and yes, the shape and size of our economy—will be profoundly shaped by the outcome of this struggle.

Given the time pressures of this project I have leant on many shoulders and it therefore gives me great pleasure to acknowledge the following debts of gratitude:

- To Tarana Burke for her inspiration and bravery. Back in 2006 she founded a nascent Me Too movement to raise awareness of the pervasiveness of sexual abuse and assault in society.
- To Jan Alexander for her research expertise and the finesse and empathy she brought to interviews.
- To Luana Pomponet for her data analytics and integration capabilities, which were critical to extracting the "new news" from a large body of complex survey material.
- To Kennedy Ihezie for his courageous thought leadership. I particularly appreciate his practical help in making sure this book reached across the divides of race and sexual orientation as well as those of gender.
- To the eighty-plus victims of sexual misconduct who had the guts—and the generosity of spirit—to tell their stories, some-

times at considerable psychic cost to themselves. Their voices thread through this book and are transformational.

- To the twenty-plus senior executives who devoted precious hours to one-on-one interviews, sharing—at a granular level— the tools and tactics they use to tamp down sexual misconduct and build more inclusive leadership cultures.

- To CTI's board, executive leadership, and best-in-class research operation.

- To Hollis Heimbouch and her extraordinary editorial team. This is the second book I've written with HarperCollins and it could not have been a better experience.

- To Molly Friedrich, my literary agent and longtime friend, who was the first to urge me to turn this research into a book; in fact she insisted on it.

Sylvia Ann Hewlett
New York City
August 2019

NOTES

Preface

1. Mahmoud Latif v. Morgan Stanley & Co., Morgan Stanley Services Group, and seven individuals. U.S. District Court, Southern District of New York. https://www.financialservicesemploymentlaw.com/files/2019/07/Latif-v -Morgan-Stanley.pdf.

Chapter 1: #MeToo: Where We're Coming from—and Going

1. Berebitsky, Julie. *Sex and the Office: A History of Gender, Power, and Desire* (New Haven and London: Yale University Press, 2012), 65.
2. Berebitsky, *Sex and the Office*, 14.
3. Lytle, Tamara. "Title VII Changed the Face of the American Workplace." *HR Magazine*. Society for Human Resource Management. May 21, 2014, https://www.shrm.org/hr-today/news/hr-magazine/pages/title-vii-changed -the-face-of-the-american-workplace.aspx.
4. MacKinnon, Catharine. *Sexual Harassment of Working Women: A Case of Sex Discrimination* (New Haven: Yale University Press, 1979), vii (foreword by Thomas I. Emerson).
5. Ibid.
6. Theunissen, Gert, Marijke Verbruggen, Anneleen Forrier, and Luc Sels. "Career Sidestep, Wage Setback? The Impact of Different Types of Employment Interruptions on Wages." Wiley Online Library. John Wiley & Sons, Ltd (10.1111), September 14, 2009, https://onlinelibrary.wiley .com/doi/abs/10.1111/j.1468-0432.2009.00471.x.
7. Totenberg, Nina. "A Timeline of Clarence Thomas-Anita Hill Controversy as Kavanaugh to Face Accuser." NPR. September 23, 2018, https://www .npr.org/2018/09/23/650138049/a-timeline-of-clarence-thomas-anita-hill -controversy-as-kavanaugh-to-face-accuse.
8. Brock, David. "Kavanaugh's Accuser Should Unfortunately Expect the Anita Hill Treatment from Republicans." NBCUniversal News Group. September

18, 2018, https://www.nbcnews.com/think/opinion/kavanaugh-s-accuser
-should-unfortunately-expect-anita-hill-treatment-republicans-ncna910226.

9. "The Starr Report, Narrative Part II: Initial Sexual Encounters," published
by the Washington Post Company, 1998, https://www.washingtonpost.com
/wp-srv/politics/special/clinton/icreport/6narrit.htm.

10. Lewinsky, Monica. "Monica Lewinsky: Emerging from 'the House of Gaslight'
in the Age of #MeToo." *Vanity Fair.* February 23, 2018, https://www.vanityfair
.com/news/2018/02/monica-lewinsky-in-the-age-of-metoo.

11. Flanagan, Caitlin. "Bill Clinton: A Reckoning." *Atlantic.* February 26, 2018.
Accessed July 16, 2019, https://www.theatlantic.com/entertainment/archive
/2017/11/reckoning-with-bill-clintons-sex-crimes/545729/.

12. Economos, Nicole. " 'I'm Not a Punchline, I'm a Human Being': Monica
Lewinsky Debuts Anti-Bullying PSA." *Sydney Morning Herald.* October 11, 2017,
https://www.smh.com.au/entertainment/celebrity/im-not-a-punchline-im
-a-human-being-monica-lewinsky-debuts-antibullying-psa-20171011-gyynt1
.html.

13. Grigoriadis, Vanessa. "Monica Takes Manhattan." *New York* magazine. March
19, 2001, http://nymag.com/nymetro/news/people/features/4481/.

14. Lang, Brent. "How *New York Times* Reporters Broke Hollywood's Biggest
Sexual Harassment Story." *Variety.* December 17, 2017, https://variety.com
/2017/biz/features/new-york-times-harvey-weinstein-report-megan-twohey
-jodi-kantor-1202637948/.

15. Farley, Lin. *Sexual Shakedown* (New York: McGraw Hill, 1978), p. 91.

16. Moniuszko, Sara M., and Cara Kelly. "Harvey Weinstein Scandal: A Complete
List of the 87 Accusers." *USA Today.* June 1, 2018. Accessed July 16, 2019,
https://www.usatoday.com/story/life/people/2017/10/27/weinstein-scandal
-complete-list-accusers/804663001/.

17. Abcarian, Robin. "California Journal: Another Man Behaving Badly in
Hollywood—This Time, Harvey Weinstein. What a Shocker." *Los Angeles Times.*
October 6, 2017. Accessed July 16, 2019, https://www.latimes.com/local
/abcarian/la-me-abcarian-weinstein-harassment-20171006-story.html.

18. Wakabayashi, Daisuke. "Google Approved $45 Million Exit Package for
Executive Accused of Misconduct." *New York Times.* March 11, 2019. Accessed
July 16, 2019, https://www.nytimes.com/2019/03/11/technology/google
-misconduct-exit-package.html.

19. Gelles, David. "Wall Street Has Been Unscathed by MeToo. Until Now."
New York Times. March 16, 2019, https://www.nytimes.com/2019/03/16
/business/metoo-wall-street-tcw-tirschwell-ravich.html.

20. Casselman, Ben, and Jim Tankersley. "Women in Economics Report Rampant Sexual Assault and Bias." *New York Times.* March 18, 2019, https://www.nytimes.com/2019/03/18/business/economy/women-economics-discrimination.html.

21. "Update on NIH's Efforts to Address Sexual Harassment in Science." National Institutes of Health, U.S. Department of Health and Human Services. March 6, 2019, https://www.nih.gov/about-nih/who-we-are/nih-director/statements/update-nihs-efforts-address-sexual-harassment-science.

22. "Poll Reveals Divided Understanding of #MeToo." NPR. October 31, 2018, https://www.npr.org/about-npr/662519588/poll-reveals-divided-understanding-of-metoo.

23. Carlsen, Audrey, et al. "#MeToo Brought Down 201 Powerful Men. Nearly Half of Their Replacements Are Women." *New York Times.* Updated October 29, 2018, https://www.nytimes.com/interactive/2018/10/23/us/metoo-replacements.html.

24. Carlsen et al., "#MeToo Brought Down 201 Powerful Men."

25. Gray, Sarah. "Amazon Studios Head Jennifer Salke Talks 'Lord of the Rings,' Sexual Harassment." *Fortune.* June 11, 2018, http://fortune.com/2018/06/11/amazon-studios-head-jennifer-salke/.

26. Donnelly, Matt, and Brett Long. "Inside Jennifer Salke's Amazon Film Shakeup." *Variety.* September 26, 2018, https://variety.com/2018/film/news/amazon-film-jennifer-salke-julie-rapaport-1202958837/.

27. "Inequality Across 1,200 Popular Films: Examining Gender and Race/Ethnicity of Leads/Co Leads from 2007 to 2018." Annenberg Inclusion Initiative. U.S.C. Annenberg, http://assets.uscannenberg.org/docs/inequality-in-1200-films-research-brief_2019-02-12.pdf.

28. Smith, Stacy L. "The Data behind Hollywood's Sexism." TED Talk on Annenberg Inclusion Initiative website, https://annenberg.usc.edu/research/aii#inequality.

29. Steel, Emily. "Costs for Fox's Harassment Settlements Rise to $50 Million." *New York Times.* August 15, 2017, https://www.nytimes.com/2017/08/14/business/media/fox-harassment-settlements-cost.html?module=inline.

30. Editorial Board. "Deloitte Helps Show the Way on Harassment." *Financial Times.* December 16, 2018, https://www.ft.com/content/95252f5c-ffa2-11e8-ac00-57a2a826423e.

31. Ibid.

32. Stein v. Knight complaint, Circuit Court of the State of Oregon for the

County of Multnomah, https://s3.amazonaws.com/arc-wordpress-client
-uploads/wweek/wp-content/uploads/2018/09/04174917/Stein-v-Knight
.pdf.

33. "Nike, Inc.—Sexual Misconduct Risk Management—(2018)." Trillium
    Asset Management. Accessed September 13, 2019, https://trilliuminvest
    .com/shareholder-proposal/nike-inc-sexual-misconduct-risk-management
    -2018/.

34. Wakabayashi, Daisuke, and Kate Conger. "Board Sued Over Google's Exit
    Package for Accused Executive." *New York Times.* January 11, 2019, https://
    www.nytimes.com/2019/01/10/technology/google-rubin-shareholder-lawsuit
    .html.

35. "CalPERS Weighs Push for Sexual-Harassment Corporate Disclosure."
    Bloomberg Law. April 11, 2018.

36. Frye, Jocelyn. "Not Just the Rich and Famous." Center for American Progress.
    November 20, 2017, https://www.americanprogress.org/issues/women/news
    /2017/11/20/443139/not-just-rich-famous/.

37. Restaurant Opportunities Centers United, Forward Together, et al. "The
    Glass Floor: Sexual Harassment in the Restaurant Industry." New York,
    NY: Restaurant Opportunities Centers United. October 7, 2014, http://
    rocunited.org/wp-content/uploads/2014/10/REPORT_TheGlassFloor
    _Sexual-Harassment-in-the-Restaurant-Industry.pdf.

38. Ryzik, Melena. "In a Test of Their Power, #MeToo's Legal Forces Take On
    McDonald's." *New York Times.* May 21, 2019, https://www.nytimes.com
    /2019/05/21/business/mcdonalds-female-employees-sexual-harassment
    .html.

39. McEnery, Thornton. "Senior Executive That Was Too Toxic for Travis
    Kalanick's Uber Finds a New Home at a Hedge Fund." *Dealbreaker.* October
    24, 2018, https://dealbreaker.com/2018/10/senior-executive-that-was-too
    -toxic-for-travis-kalanicks-uber-finds-a-new-home-at-a-hedge-fund.

40. Tan, Gillian, and Katia Porzecanski. "Wall Street Rule for the #MeToo Era:
    Avoid Women at All Cost." Bloomberg News. December 3, 2018, https://
    www.bloomberg.com/news/articles/2018-12-03/a-wall-street-rule-for-the
    -metoo-era-avoid-women-at-all-cost.

41. Ibid.

42. Center for Talent Innovation. "What "MeToo Means for Corporate
    America." July 2018.

43. Deb, Sopan. "Woody Allen Sues Amazon Over Canceled $68 Million Deal."

New York Times. February 7, 2019, https://www.nytimes.com/2019/02/07 /movies/woody-allen-amazon-lawsuit.html.

44. "McCann Health: Advertising & Marketing Assignments," https://www .adbrands.net/us/mccann-health-us.htm.

45. United States Supreme Court, *Meritor Savings Bank v. Vinson* (1986), No. 84–1979, Decided: June 19, 1986, https://caselaw.findlaw.com/us-supreme -court/477/57.html.

46. United States Court of Appeals, Ninth Circuit, Brooks v. City of San Mateo, No. 98–15818, Decided: June 5, 2000, https://caselaw.findlaw.com/us-9th -circuit/1013868.html.

47. Lee, Edmund, and Rachel Abrams. "CBS Says Les Moonves Will Not Receive $120 Million Severance." *New York Times*. December 17, 2018, https://www .nytimes.com/2018/12/17/business/media/les-moonves-cbs-severance.html.

48. "EEOC Releases Fiscal Year 2018 Enforcement and Litigation Data," press release from EEOC, April 10, 2019, https://www.eeoc.gov/eeoc/newsroom /release/4-10-19.cfm.

Chapter 2: Measuring and Mapping

1. Hewlett, Sylvia Ann, et al. "The Sponsor Effect: Breaking Through the Last Glass Ceiling." *Harvard Business Review Research Report*. December 2010.

2. Phillips & Associates. "2016 Marks the 20th Anniversary of a Groundbreaking Wall Street Sexual Harassment Lawsuit—New York Employment Attorney Blog—October 24, 2016." New York Employment Attorney Blog. July 5, 2018, https://www.newyorkemploymentattorney -blog.com/2016-marks-20th-anniversary-groundbreaking-wall-street -sexual-harassment-lawsuit/.

3. McCoy, Kevin. "Sexual Harassment: Here Are Some of the Biggest Cases." *USA Today*. October 25, 2017. Accessed July 16, 2019, https://www.usatoday .com/story/money/2017/10/25/sexual-harassment-here-some-biggest-cases /791439001/.

4. Lipman, Joanne. "What *The Wolf of Wall Street* Is Missing: The Women." *Time*. December 30, 2013, http://entertainment.time.com/2013/12/30/what -the-wolf-of-wall-street-is-missing-the-women/.

5. "EEOC Select Task Force on the Study of Harassment in the Workplace." EEOC. June 20, 2016, https://www.eeoc.gov/eeoc/task_force/harassment /report.cfm#_Toc453686305.

Chapter 3: Women as Predators

1. "Overview of Title IX of the Education Amendments of 1972, 20 U.S.C. A§ 1681 Et. Seq." The United States Department of Justice. August 7, 2015, https://www.justice.gov/crt/overview-title-ix-education-amendments-1972-20-usc-1681-et-seq.

2. Reitman, Nimrod. Plaintiff, against Avita Ronell and New York University, Supreme Court of the State of New York County of New York, August 16, 2018, https://blog.simplejustice.us/wp-content/uploads/2018/08/FINAL-Complaint-Reitman-v.-Ronell-and-NYU.pdf.

3. Greenberg, Zoe. "What Happens to #MeToo When a Feminist Is the Accused?" *New York Times.* August 13, 2018, https://www.nytimes.com/2018/08/13/nyregion/sexual-harassment-nyu-female-professor.html.

4. Ibid.

5. "Blaming the Victim Is Apparently OK When the Accused in a Title IX Proceeding Is a Feminist Literary Theorist." Leiter Reports: A Philosophy Blog. Accessed September 13, 2019, https://leiterreports.typepad.com/blog/2018/06/blaming-the-victim-is-apparently-ok-when-the-accused-is-a-feminist-literary-theorist.html.

6. O'Hehir, Andrew. "When a Woman Is Accused of Sexual Misconduct: The Strange Case of Avital Ronell." *Salon.* August 20, 2018, https://www.salon.com/2018/08/18/when-a-woman-is-accused-of-sexual-misconduct-the-strange-case-of-avital-ronell/.

7. Severson, Kim. "Asia Argento, a #MeToo Leader, Made a Deal With Her Own Accuser." *New York Times.* August 20, 2018, https://www.nytimes.com/2018/08/19/us/asia-argento-assault-jimmy-bennett.html.

8. Ryan, Lisa. "The Asia Argento Sexual-Assault Case Keeps Getting More Complicated." *The Cut.* September 17, 2018, https://www.thecut.com/2018/09/asia-argento-sexual-assault-what-to-know.html.

9. Miller, Julie. "Asia Argento Details Alleged Assault by Jimmy Bennett; Asks *X Factor Italy* to Rehire Her." *Vanity Fair.* October 1, 2018, https://www.vanityfair.com/hollywood/2018/10/asia-argento-jimmy-bennett-italian-interview.

10. Severson, Kim. "Asia Argento, a #MeToo Leader, Made a Deal With Her Own Accuser." *New York Times.* August 20, 2018, https://www.nytimes.com/2018/08/19/us/asia-argento-assault-jimmy-bennett.html.

11. Hakim, Catherine. *Erotic Capital: The Power of Attraction in the Boardroom and the Bedroom* (New York: Basic Books, 2011).

12. Ibid.
13. Persaud, MD, Raj, and Peter Bruggen, MD. "What Is the Link Between Sex and Power in Sexual Harassment?" *Psychology Today.* November 8, 2017, https://www.psychologytoday.com/us/blog/slightly-blighty/201711/what -is-the-link-between-sex-and-power-in-sexual-harassment.
14. Hancock, David. "Clinton Cheated 'Because I Could.'" CBS News. June 16, 2004, https://www.cbsnews.com/news/clinton-cheated-because-i-could -16-06-2004/.
15. Kunstman, Jonathan W., and Jon K. Maner. "Sexual Overperception: Power, Mating Motives, and Biases in Social Judgment." *Journal of Personality and Social Psychology.* December 13, 2010, https://cms.qz.com/wp-content/uploads /2018/01/83e41-sexual-overperception.pdf.
16. LaSalle, Mick. "Film Review—'Disclosure' Features Sexual Harassment With a Twist." *San Francisco Chronicle.* February 4, 2012, https://www.sfgate .com/movies/article/Film Review-Disclosure-Features-Sexual-3030256 .php.
17. Moyer, Justin Wm. "A Look Back at 'Disclosure': Does Hollywood Prefer Films about Women Sexually Harassing Men?" *Washington Post.* December 22, 2017, https://www.washingtonpost.com/entertainment/a-look-back-at -disclosure-does-hollywood-prefer-films-about-women-sexually-harassing -men/2017/12/21/cb52df6e-d156-11e7-9129-83c7078d23cb_story.html.
18. Malone, Noreen. "Former Thinx Employee Accuses Miki Agrawal of Sexual Harassment." *The Cut.* March 20, 2017, https://www.thecut.com/2017/03 /thinx-employee-accuses-miki-agrawal-of-sexual-harassment.html.
19. Malone, Noreen. "Sexual Harassment Claims Against a 'She-E.-O.'" *The Cut.* NYMag.com. March 2017, https://www.thecut.com/2017/03/thinx -employee-accuses-miki-agrawal-of-sexual-harassment.html.
20. Stemple, Lara, and Ilan H Meyer. "The Sexual Victimization of Men in America: New Data Challenge Old Assumptions." *American Journal of Public Health.* American Public Health Association. June 2014, https:// www.ncbi.nlm.nih.gov/pmc/articles/PMC4062022/.
21. Stemple, Lara, and Ilan H. Meyer. "Sexual Victimization by Women Is More Common Than Previously Known." *Scientific American.* October 10, 2017, https://www.scientificamerican.com/article/sexual-victimization-by -women-is-more-common-than-previously-known/.
22. Bodenner, Chris. "When a Woman Sexually Assaults a Man." *Atlantic.* December 1, 2016, https://www.theatlantic.com/notes/2016/11/australia /509120/.

23. Lafave, Debra. "Why We Can't See Women as Sexual Predators, and Why It Matters." *Medium*. September 12, 2017, https://medium.com/s/all-rise /debra-lafave-why-we-cant-see-women-as-sexual-predators-and-why-it -matters-7984bd98b184.

Chapter 4: Men as Prey

1. Lebrecht, Norman. "Some Thoughts on James Levine's $27,000 Nightly Rate." *Slipped Disc*. Accessed September 13, 2019, https://slippedisc.com /2018/05/some-thoughts-on-james-levines-27000-nightly-rate/.
2. Cooper, Michael. "Met Opera Reels as Fourth Man Accuses James Levine of Sexual Abuse." *New York Times*. December 5, 2017, https://www .nytimes.com/2017/12/04/arts/music/james-levine-met-opera.html.
3. Gay, Malcolm. "Metropolitan Opera Terminates Relationship with James Levine over 'Sexually Abusive' Conduct." *Boston Globe*. March 13, 2018, https:// www.bostonglobe.com/arts/music/2018/03/12/metlevine/zqUkJyq1D7P4r xruzrHTCJ/story.html.
4. Caniglia, John, and Jo Ellen Corrigan. "Two Former Students Accuse Conductor James Levine of Sexually Abusing Them in Cleveland." Cleveland .com. December 6, 2017, https://www.cleveland.com/metro/2017/12/two _former_students_accuse_con.html.
5. Cooper, Michael. "Met Opera Reels as Fourth Man Accuses James Levine of Sexual Abuse." *New York Times*. December 5, 2017, https://www .nytimes.com/2017/12/04/arts/music/james-levine-met-opera.html.
6. Schipp, Debbie. "'Cult' Members' Awful Choice." News.Com.Au. July 16, 2018, https://www.news.com.au/world/north-america/awful-choice -inside-the-cult-of-conductor-james-levine/news-story/28b101aece0270ba 549adffdbf97d68f.
7. Cooper, Michael. "Met Opera Suspends James Levine After New Sexual Abuse Accusations." *New York Times*. December 4, 2017, https://www .nytimes.com/2017/12/03/arts/music/james-levine-met-opera.html.
8. Ibid.
9. Andrews, Travis M. "Met Opera's James Levine, Once 'America's Top Maestro,' Is Finished, after Investigation Finds Years of 'Sexually Abusive' Conduct." *Washington Post*. March 13, 2018, https://www.washingtonpost .com/news/morning-mix/wp/2018/03/13/the-metropolitan-operas-james -levine-once-on-the-cover-of-time-has-been-fired-for-alleged-sexual-abuse/.

10. Morral, Andrew R., Kristie L. Gore, Terry L. Schell (editors). *Sexual Assault and Sexual Harassment in the US Military*, volume 2 from the 2014 RAND Military Workplace Study (Santa Monica: RAND corporation, 2015), p. 27.

11. Hurley, Parker. "I'm a Male Model, and I'm Coming Forward About Bruce Weber." *Racked*. February 28, 2018, https://www.racked.com/2018/2/28 /17053684/bruce-weber-male-model.

12. Ibid.

13. Noam Galai/Getty. "'You Could Have Just Beat Him Up. Why Didn't You?'." *The Cut*. January 25, 2018, https://www.thecut.com/2018/01/fashion -photographer-bruce-weber-sexual-assault.html?utm_campaign=thecut&utm _source=tw&utm_medium=s1.

14. "Male Sexual Assault: Issues of Arousal and Consent." *Cleveland State University Law Review* Vol 51, p 95 (2004), https://engagedscholarship .csuohio.edu/cgi/viewcontent.cgi?article=1305&context=clevstlrev.

15. Weiss, Karen G. "Male Sexual Victimization." *Men and Masculinities* 12, no. 3 (August 2008): 275–98, https://doi.org/10.1177/1097184x0832 2632.

16. Scalia. "Oncale v. Sundowner Offshore Services, Inc., 523 U.S. 75 (1998)." Legal Information Institute. Legal Information Institute, March 4, 1998, https://www.law.cornell.edu/supct/html/96-568.ZO.html.

17. Ibid.

18. 2014 RAND Military Workplace Study Team pp. 27–29.

19. Ibid.

20. Holland, Kathryn J., Verónica Caridad Rabelo, Amber M. Gustafson, Rita C. Seabrook, and Lilia M. Cortina. "Sexual Harassment against Men: Examining the Roles of Feminist Activism, Sexuality, and Organizational Context." *Psychology of Men & Masculinity* 17, no. 1 (2016): 17–29, https:// doi.org/10.1037/a0039151.

21. Stevenson, Alexandra, and Matthew Goldstein. "Bridgewater's Ray Dalio Spreads His Gospel of 'Radical Transparency'." *New York Times*. September 8, 2017, https://www.nytimes.com/2017/09/08/business/dealbook/ bridgewaters-ray-dalio-spreads-his-gospel-of-radical-transparency.html.

22. Stevenson, Alexandra, and Matthew Goldstein. "At World's Largest Hedge Fund, Sex, Fear and Video Surveillance." *New York Times*. July 27, 2016, https://www.nytimes.com/2016/07/27/business/dealbook/bridgewater -associates-hedge-fund-culture-ray-dalio.html.

23. 2014 RAND Military Workplace Study Team, p. 50.

Chapter 5: Crossing Lines of Race and Sexual Orientation

1. Patrick, Kris. "Terry & Rebecca Crews Talk Hardships and Faith in Holllywood." *Path MEGAzine*. April 2, 2013, http://pathmegazine.com/articles/cover-stories/actor-terry-crews-explains-how-he-does-everything-unto-the-lord-in-hollywood/.

2. Kindelan, Katie, and Sabina Ghebremedhin. "Terry Crews Names Alleged Sexual Assaulter: 'I Will Not Be Shamed.'" ABC News *Good Morning America*. November 15, 2017, https://abcnews.go.com/Entertainment/terry-crews-names-alleged-sexual-assaulter-shamed/story?id=51146972.

3. "Terry Crews Testifies on Survivors' Bill of Rights." C-Span. Accessed September 13, 2019, https://www.c-span.org/video/?447596-1/terry-crews-testifies-survivors-bill-rights.

4. Dockterman, Eliana. "Terry Crews: 'Men Need to Hold Other Men Accountable.'" *Time*. December 16, 2017, http://time.com/5049671/terry-crews-interview-transcript-person-of-the-year-2017/.

5. Wingfield, Adia Harvey. "When Black Men Are Harassed." *Slate*. May 8, 2018, https://slate.com/human-interest/2018/05/when-black-men-are-harassed-at-work.html.

6. Wingfield, Adia Harvey. "Are Some Emotions Marked 'Whites Only'? Racialized Feeling Rules in Professional Workplaces." *Social Problems* 57, no. 2 (2010): 251-68.

7. Morris, Wesley. "Why Pop Culture Just Can't Deal With Black Male Sexuality." *New York Times*. October 27, 2016, https://www.nytimes.com/interactive/2016/10/30/magazine/black-male-sexuality-last-taboo.html.

8. Hirsch, Afua. "'As a Black Woman I'm Always Fetishised': Racism in the Bedroom." *Guardian*. January 13, 2018, https://www.theguardian.com/lifeandstyle/2018/jan/13/black-woman-always-fetishised-racism-in-bedroom.

9. Crenshaw, Kimberlé. "Demarginalizing the Intersection of Race and Sex: A Black Feminist Critique of Antidiscrimination Doctrine, Feminist Theory and Antiracist Politics," *University of Chicago Legal Forum*, 1989, issue 1, article 8, https://chicagounbound.uchicago.edu/cgi/viewcontent.cgi?referer=&httpsredir=1&article=1052&context=uclf.

10. Buchanan, NiCole, and Louise Fitzgerald. "Effects of Racial and Sexual Harassment on Work and the Psychological Well-Being of African American Women." *Journal of Occupational Health Psychology* 2008, vol. 13, no. 2, 137-51.

11. Caulfield, Sueann, and Cristiana Schettini. "Gender and Sexuality in

Brazil since Independence." *Oxford Research Encyclopedias.* Latin American History, http://oxfordre.com/latinamericanhistory/view/10.1093/acrefore /9780199366439.001.0001/acrefore-9780199366439-e-296.

12. Suero, Waleska. "We Don't Think of It as Sexual Harassment." *Chicana(o)/ Latina(o) Law Review,* 33(1), 2015. Suero was a JD candidate at Georgetown University at the time of publication; she is now a lawyer with the office of the Bronx District Attorney.

13. Branson-Potts, Hailey. "Gay Mayor Accused of Sexual Harassment as #MeToo Reckoning Comes to West Hollywood." *Los Angeles Times.* February 16, 2019, https://www.latimes.com/local/lanow/la-me-ln-weho-sexual-scandal -protests-20190216-story.html.

14. Liptak, Adam. "Supreme Court to Decide Whether Landmark Civil Rights Law Applies to Gay and Transgender Workers." *New York Times.* April 22, 2019, https://www.nytimes.com/2019/04/22/us/politics/supreme-court-gay-transgender -employees.html?action=click&module=Well&pgtype=Homepage§ion.

15. Jeffrey A. Willy v. Eli Lilly and Company, United States District Court, Southern District of Indiana, Indianapolis Division, filed December 14, 2018, https://ia801505.us.archive.org/34/items/gov.uscourts.insd.90117 /gov.uscourts.insd.90117.1.0.pdf.

Chapter 6: Hits to the Bottom Line

1. Finley, Nolan. "Finley: MSU Cost in Gymnast Abuse Scandal Could Top $1B." *Detroit News.* December 3, 2017, https://www.detroitnews.com/story /opinion/columnists/nolan-finley/2017/12/02/cost-msu-gymnast-scandal /108247652/.

2. Major Sexual Abuse Settlements in the Catholic Church. Accessed September 16, 2019, https://www.bishop-accountability.org/settlements/.

3. Steel, Emily. "Costs for Fox's Harassment Settlements Rise to $50 Million." *New York Times.* August 15, 2017, https://www.nytimes.com/2017/08/14 /business/media/fox-harassment-settlements-cost.html?module=inline.

4. Steel, Emily. "Fox Settles Discrimination Lawsuits for Roughly $10 Million." *New York Times.* May 15, 2018, https://www.nytimes.com/2018/05/15 /business/media/fox-news-discrimination-lawsuits.html.

5. Milford, Maureen. "Judge Approves $90 Million Fox 21st Century Sexual Harassment Settlement." https://www.directorsandboards.com/news/judge -approves-90-million-fox-sexual-harassment-settlement.

6. Wakabayashi, Daisuke. "Google Approved $45 Million Exit Package for

Executive Accused of Misconduct." *New York Times*. https://www.nytimes
.com/2019/03/11/technology/google-misconduct-exit-package.html.

7. Carr, Flora. "Former Google Employee Hits Tech Giant With a Sexual
Harassment Lawsuit Alleging 'Bro Culture.'" *Fortune*. March 1, 2018,
http://fortune.com/2018/03/01/google-sexual-harassment-lawsuit-bro
-culture/.

8. Baron, Ethan. "Google's Parent Firm Alphabet Lost Billions through
Response to Sexual Harassment: Lawsuit." *Mercury News*. January 11, 2019,
https://www.mercurynews.com/2019/01/10/googles-parent-firm-alphabet
-lost-billions-through-response-to-sexual-harassment-lawsuit/.

9. Safronova, Valeriya. "Paul Marciano Will Leave Guess After Sexual
Harassment Settlements." *New York Times*. June 12, 2018, https://www
.nytimes.com/2018/06/12/style/guess-harassment-resignation.html.

10. Steel, Emily. "At Vice, Cutting-Edge Media and Allegations of Old-School
Sexual Harassment." *New York Times*. December 23, 2017, https://www
.nytimes.com/2017/12/23/business/media/vice-sexual-harassment.html?_r=0.

11. McCoy, Kevin. "Sexual Harassment: Here Are Some of the Biggest Cases."
USA Today. October 25, 2017, https://www.usatoday.com/story/money/2017
/10/25/sexual-harassment-here-some-biggest-cases/791439001/.

12. Copeland, Rob. "Google Agreed to Pay $135 Million to Two Executives
Accused of Sexual Harassment." *Wall Street Journal*. March 12, 2019,
https://www.wsj.com/articles/google-agreed-to-pay-135-million-to-two
-executives-accused-of-sexual-harassment-11552334653.

13. Feldblum, Chai, and Victoria Lipnic. "Select Task Force on the Study of
Harassment in the Workplace." U.S. Equal Employment Opportunity
Comission, n.d., 18.

14. Tippett, Elizabeth C. "Nike's #MeToo Moment Shows How 'Legal'
Harassment Can Lead to Illegal Discrimination." *The Conversation*.
November 14, 2018, https://theconversation.com/nikes-metoo-moment
-shows-how-legal-harassment-can-lead-to-illegal-discrimination-95828.

15. Lawrence, Dune. "To Sue Goldman Sachs, You Have to Be Willing to Hang
On—For a Long, Long Time." Bloomberg. Accessed September 13, 2019,
https://www.bloomberg.com/news/features/2018-05-03/wall-street-s
-biggest-gender-lawsuit-is-13-years-in-the-making.

16. Tippett, Elizabeth Chika. "The Legal Implications of the MeToo
Movement." *Minnesota Law Review*, p, 43. July 17, 2018. Available at SSRN:
https://ssrn.com/abstract=3170764.

17. Jinolabs. "EY partner Don Manifold leaves the firm over code of

conduct breach." Accessed September 16, 2019, https://jinolabs.com/article/86611745/ey-partner-don-manifold-leaves-the-firm-over-code-of.

18. "Mitsubishi Motor Manufacturing and EEOC Reach Voluntary Agreement to Settle Harassment Suit." Accessed September 13, 2019, https://www.eeoc.gov/eeoc/newsroom/release/6-11-98.cfm.

19. "Top Court Backs Kaiyukan on Sex Harassment Suspensions." *The Japan Times*. https://www.japantimes.co.jp/news/2015/02/26/national/crime-legal/top-court-backs-kaiyukan-on-sex-harassment-suspensions/.

20. "Japanese Court Upholds Penalties for Sexual Harassment." *The National Law Review*. Accessed September 16, 2019, https://www.natlawreview.com/article/japanese-court-upholds-penalties-sexual-harassment.

21. Rubin, Alissa J. "'Revolt' in France Against Sexual Harassment Hits Cultural Resistance." *New York Times*. November 19, 2017, https://www.nytimes.com/2017/11/19/world/europe/france-sexual-harassment.html/.

22. Rubin, Alissa J., and Elian Peltier. "Employees of Big French Cleaning Company Win Sexual Harassment Case." *New York Times*. November 11, 2017, https://www.nytimes.com/2017/11/10/world/europe/sexual-harassment-france-h-reinier.html/.

23. Castro, and Luciano Guaraldo. "Após 35 Anos, Globo Dispensa José Mayer, Acusado De Assédio Sexual." Notícias da TV. January 15, 2019, https://noticiasdatv.uol.com.br/noticia/celebridades/apos-35-anos-globodispensa-jose-mayer-acusado-de-assedio-sexual-24359#idc-cover.

24. Kunstman, Jonathan W., and Jon K. Maner. "Sexual Overperception: Power, Mating Motives, and Biases in Social Judgment." Northwestern Scholars. American Psychological Association Inc., March 19, 2016, https://www.scholars.northwestern.edu/en/publications/sexual-overperception-power-mating-motives-and-biases-in-social-j.

25. Roeder, Tom. "That Air Force Academy Hazing Ritual Was Like Something Out of a Bad Fraternity Movie." Task & Purpose. April 15, 2019, https://taskandpurpose.com/air-force-academy-hazing-ritual.

26. Desta, Yohana. "After Months-Long Death Rattles, the Weinstein Company Is Officially Kaput." *Vanity Fair*. July 16, 2018, https://www.vanityfair.com/hollywood/2018/07/the-weinstein-company-lantern-entertainment.

27. Moniuszko, Sara M., and Cara Kelly. "Harvey Weinstein Scandal: A Complete List of the 87 Accusers." *USA Today*. June 1, 2018, https://www.usatoday.com/story/life/people/2017/10/27/weinstein-scandal-complete-list-accusers/804663001/.

28. Barnes, Brooks. "Weinstein Company Files for Bankruptcy and Revokes

Nondisclosure Agreements." *New York Times*. March 20, 2018, https://
www.nytimes.com/2018/03/19/business/weinstein-company-bankruptcy
.html.

29. Carroll, Rory, and Sam Levin. "'Pack of Hyenas': How Harvey Weinstein's
Power Fuelled a Culture of Enablers." *Guardian*. October 13, 2017. https://
www.theguardian.com/film/2017/oct/13/harvey-weinstein-allegations
-hollywood-enablers.

30. Hayes, Dade, Dawn C. Chmielewski, and Dominic Patten. "Les Moonves
Leaves Complicated Legacy at CBS as Company and Industry Look to
Emerge from His Long Shadow." *Deadline*. September 10, 2018, https://
deadline.com/2018/09/les-moonves-leaves-complicated-legacy-at-cbs
-1202460800/.

31. Stewart, James. "'Disaster for CBS Shareholders': Damning Report on
Moonves Reveals Total Failure at Top." *New York Times*. December 5, 2018,
https://www.nytimes.com/2018/12/04/business/leslie-moonves-cbs-board
.html.

32. Benner, Katie. "A Backlash Builds Against Sexual Harassment in Silicon Valley."
New York Times. July 4, 2017, https://www.nytimes.com/2017/07/03/technology
/silicon-valley-sexual-harassment.html; Albergotti, Reed, Michealene Risley,
and Jonathan Kim. "Silicon Valley Women Tell of VC's Unwanted Advances."
The Information. https://www.theinformation.com/articles/silicon-valley
-women-tell-of-vcs-unwanted-advances.

33. Guynn, Jessica. "Venture Capitalist Steve Jurvetson Resigns from Firm,
Takes Leave from Tesla, SpaceX Boards." *USA Today*. November 15, 2017,
https://www.usatoday.com/story/tech/2017/11/13/steve-jurvetson-out-dfj
-amid-harassment-probe/859757001/.

34. Kovach, Steve. "Shervin Pishevar, Accused of Sexual Misconduct by 6
Women, Resigns from Sherpa Capital." *Business Insider*. December 14,
2017, https://www.businessinsider.com/shervin-pishevar-resigns-sherpa-
capital-sexual-misconduct-allegations-2017-12.

35. Grind, Kirsten, and Sarah Krouse. "Star Fidelity Manager Gavin Baker Fired
Over Sexual Harassment Allegations." *Wall Street Journal*. October 12, 2017,
https://www.wsj.com/articles/star-fidelity-manager-gavin-baker-fired-over
-sexual-harassment-allegations-1507841061.

36. Creswell, Julie, and Kevin Draper. "5 More Nike Executives Are Out Amid
Inquiry Into Harassment Allegations." *New York Times*. May 8, 2018,
https://www.nytimes.com/2018/05/08/business/nike-harassment.html.

37. Fowler, Susan. "Reflecting on One Very, Very Strange Year at Uber." Susan

Fowler. February 19, 2017, https://www.susanjfowler.com/blog/2017/2/19/reflecting-on-one-very-strange-year-at-uber.

38. Solon, Olivia. "Uber Fires More than 20 Employees after Sexual Harassment Investigation." *Guardian.* June 7, 2017, https://www.theguardian.com/technology/2017/jun/06/uber-fires-employees-sexual-harassment-investigation.

39. Wieczner, Jen. "Uber's Stock Was Sinking Even Before CEO Travis Kalanick Resigned." *Fortune.* June 23, 2017, http://fortune.com/2017/06/23/uber-stock-ceo-travis-kalanick-t-rowe-price/.

40. Kosoff, Maya. "Uber Gets a $20 Billion Reality Check." *Vanity Fair.* November 28, 2017, https://www.vanityfair.com/news/2017/11/uber-gets-a-20-billion-dollar-reality-check.

41. Bhuiyan, Johana. "With Just Her Words, Susan Fowler Brought Uber to Its Knees." *Vox.* December 6, 2017, https://www.recode.net/2017/12/6/16680602/susan-fowler-uber-engineer-recode-100-diversity-sexual-harassment.

42. Wolverton, Troy. "Sure, Uber Didn't Leave Any Money on the Table, but Its IPO Was Nothing to Celebrate and It Could Haunt the Company and Its Execs for Years to Come." *Business Insider.* Accessed September 13, 2019, https://markets.businessinsider.com/news/stocks/why-uber-disappointing-ipo-could-haunt-company-for-years-2019-5-1028191409.

43. Kerr, Dara. "Uber CEO Dara Khosrowshahi Is Working to Clean House in Travis Kalanick's Wake." CNET. April 27, 2018, https://www.cnet.com/news/ubers-u-turn-how-ceo-dara-khosrowshahi-is-cleaning-up-after-scandals-and-lawsuits/.

44. "Uber CEO Dara Khosrowshahi Reflects on One Year at the Company." CNNMoney. August 29, 2018, https://money.cnn.com/2018/08/29/technology/uber-ceo-dara-khosrowshahi-one-year-anniversary/index.html.

45. Berzon, Alexandra, Chris Kirkham, Elizabeth Bernstein, and Kate O'Keeffe. "Dozens of People Recount Pattern of Sexual Misconduct by Las Vegas Mogul Steve Wynn." *Wall Street Journal.* January 27, 2018, https://www.wsj.com/articles/dozens-of-people-recount-pattern-of-sexual-misconduct-by-las-vegas-mogul-steve-wynn-1516985953.

46. Shen, Lucinda. "Wynn Resorts Loses $3.5 Billion After Sexual Harassment Allegations Surface About Steve Wynn." *Fortune.* January 29, 2018, https://fortune.com/2018/01/29/steve-wynn-stock-net-worth-sexual-misconduct.

47. Astor, Maggie, and Julie Creswell. "Steve Wynn Resigns from Company Amid Sexual Misconduct Allegations." *New York Times.* February 7, 2018, https://www.nytimes.com/2018/02/06/business/steve-wynn-resigns.html.

48. Ross, Katherine. "CBS Shares Fall Amid Moonves Sexual Misconduct

Allegations." *TheStreet.* July 27, 2018, https://www.thestreet.com/markets /cbs-tanks-on-speculation-of-new-yorker-expose-on-ceo-leslie-moonevs -14664951.

49. "Investors Say 'Us Too' in Wake of Sexual Misconduct Claims." Law360. https://www.law360.com/articles/1124440/investors-say-us-too-in-wake -of-sexual-misconduct-claims.

50. Fortado, Lindsay. "Women-Led Hedge Funds Try to Crack the Boys' Club." *Financial Times.* May 16, 2019, https://www.ft.com/content/73698e76- 7293-11e9-bf5c-6eeb837566c5.

51. "Tech Leavers." Kapor Center. https://www.kaporcenter.org/tech-leavers/.

52. Segarra, Lisa Marie. "More Than 20,000 Employees Participated in Google Walkout, Organizers Say." *Fortune.* November 3, 2018, http://fortune.com /2018/11/03/google-employees-walkout-demands/.

53. Hewlett, Sylvia Ann, et al., "The Sponsor Effect."

54. "Report: The Bottom Line: Connecting Corporate Performance and Gender Diversity." Catalyst, https://www.catalyst.org/research/the-bottom-line -connecting-corporate-performance-and-gender-diversity/.

55. "Gender Diversity, a Corporate Performance Driver." McKinsey & Company, https://www.mckinsey.com/business-functions/organization/our-insights /gender-diversity-a-corporate-performance-driver.

56. "Higher Returns with Women in Decision-Making Positions." Credit Suisse, https://www.credit-suisse.com/corporate/en/articles/news-and-expertise /higher-returns-with-women-in-decision-making-positions-201610.html.

57. "Gender Equality Index." Bloomberg. Accessed September 16, 2019, https:// www.bloomberg.com/gei.

58. "Linking Gender Diversity & Market Returns." Morgan Stanley. Accessed September 16, 2019, https://www.morganstanley.com/ideas/gender-diversity -investment-framework.

59. Hewlett, Sylvia Ann, Melinda Marshall, and Laura Sherbin with Tara Gonsalves. *Innovation, Diversity, and Market Growth.* (New York: Center for Talent Innovation, 2013), p. 4, Executive Summary.

60. Hewlett, Sylvia Ann et al. *Innovation, Diversity, and Market Growth*, p. 19.

61. Kristof, Nicholas. "Navigating the Male-Female Work Relationship." *New York Times.* February 13, 2019, https://www.nytimes.com/2019/02/13 /opinion/me-too-male-bosses.html.

62. "National Tracking Poll 180313." Morning Consult, n.d. https://morning consult.com/wp-content/uploads/2018/03/180313_crosstabs_vox_all -women-1.pdf.

63. Bennhold, Katrin. "Another Side of #MeToo: Male Managers Fearful of Mentoring Women." *New York Times.* January 27, 2019, https://www.nytimes.com/2019/01/27/world/europe/metoo-backlash-gender-equality-davos-men.html.

64. "The World's Most Valuable Brands." *Forbes.* https://www.forbes.com/powerful-brands/list/#tab:rank.

65. Does, Serena, Seval Gundemir, and Margaret Shih. "Research: How Sexual Harassment Affects a Company's Public Image." *Harvard Business Review.* June 13, 2018, https://hbr.org/2018/06/research-how-sexual-harassment-affects-a-companys-public-image; McGregor, Jena. "Just One Sexual Harassment Claim Can Tarnish a Company's Image." *Washington Post.* July 3, 2018, https://www.washingtonpost.com/news/on-leadership/wp/2018/07/03/how-just-one-sexual-harassment-claim-can-tarnish-a-companys-image/?utm_term=.7d23df060a41.

66. Gundemir, Seval, Serena Does, Margaret Shih. "Public Backlash Against Sexual Harassment and What Organizations Can Do About It." https://ucla.app.box.com/s/poine7tleo759nhwdz7lohy2cgk9t10v.

67. Mangan, Dan. "Suit Claims Lululemon Worker Raped by Boss after Company Created 'Perfect Environment' for Sex Predator." CNBC. December 20, 2017, https://www.cnbc.com/2017/12/20/suit-claims-lululemon-supervisor-raped-worker.html.

68. Stone, Michael. "Damaging the Brand Message . . . from Within." *Forbes.* October 31, 2018, https://www.forbes.com/sites/michaelstone/2018/02/22/damaging-the-brand-message-from-within/#39c34656144a.

69. "'Women Are Devalued and Demeaned' at Nike, Two Ex-employees Say." CNNMoney. August 10, 2018, https://money.cnn.com/2018/08/10/news/companies/nike-gender-discrimination-bias-lawsuit/index.html.

70. Goodstein, Laurie, and Sharon Otterman. "Catholic Priests Abused 1,000 Children in Pennsylvania, Report Says." *New York Times.* August 14, 2018, https://www.nytimes.com/2018/08/14/us/catholic-church-sex-abuse-pennsylvania.html.

71. Zauzmer, Julie, Michelle Boorstein, and Michael Brice-Saddler. "'Wasted Our Lives': Catholic Sex Abuse Scandals Again Prompt a Crisis of Faith." *Washington Post.* August 19, 2018, https://www.washingtonpost.com/news/acts-of-faith/wp/2018/08/19/wasted-our-lives-catholic-sex-abuse-scandals-again-prompt-a-crisis-of-faith/?utm_term=.4928fba6aa6c.

72. "Presidents Club to Close after Sexual Harassment Exposé." *Financial Times.* January 24, 2018, https://www.ft.com/content/d00e9f82-012d-11e8-9650-9c0ad2d7c5b5.

73. Lieber, Chavie. "Topshop Billionaire Philip Green Is at the Center of a #MeToo Scandal." *Vox*. October 25, 2018, https://www.vox.com/the-goods /2018/10/25/18024504/philip-green-topshop-sexual-harassment-claims -metoo.

74. Peoples, Steve. "Sexual Harassment Complaints Threaten to Derail Bernie Sanders' Bid for President in 2020." *National Post*. January 3, 2019, https:// nationalpost.com/news/world/sanders-allies-contrite-defiant-amid-harassment -allegations.

75. Creswell, Julie, Kevin Draper, and Rachel Abrams. "At Nike, Revolt Led by Women Leads to Exodus of Male Executives." *New York Times*. April 28, 2018, https://www.nytimes.com/2018/04/28/business/nike-women.html.

76. Creswell, Julie, and Kevin Draper. "5 More Nike Executives Are Out Amid Inquiry Into Harassment Allegations."

77. Greenfield, Rebecca, and Eban Novy-Williams. Bloomberg.com. August 30, 2018, https://www.bloomberg.com/news/articles/2018–08–30/nike-gets -tripped-up-while-trying-to-change-its-culture.

78. Creswell, Julie, Kevin Draper, and Rachel Abrams. "At Nike, Revolt Led by Women Leads to Exodus of Male Executives."

79. Creswell, Julie, Kevin Draper, and Rachel Abrams. "At Nike, Revolt Led by Women Leads to Exodus of Male Executives."

80. "'Women Are Devalued and Demeaned' at Nike, Two Ex-employees Say."

81. Germano, Sara, and Joann S. Lublin. "Inside Nike, a Boys-Club Culture and Flawed HR." *Wall Street Journal*. April 1, 2018, https:// www.wsj.com/articles/inside-nike-a-boys-club-culture-and-flawed-hr- 1522509975?mod=article_inline.

82. Zetlin, Minda. "Women at Nike Fight Hostile Culture with a Simple but Effective Tool That You Can Use Too." Inc.com. April 30, 2018, https:// www.inc.com/minda-zetlin/nike-sexual-harassment-survey-gender-bias- executives-fired-trevor-edwards.html.

83. "The World's Most Valuable Brands." *Forbes*, https://www.forbes.com/ powerful-brands/list/#tab:rank.

84. Kish, Matthew. "New Lawsuit Targets Phil Knight, Nike Board over 'Boys' Club' Culture." Bizjournals.com. Accessed September 16, 2019, https:// www.Bizjournals.com/portland/news/2018/09/04/new-lawsuit-targets- phil-knight-nike-board-over.html.

Chapter 7: Legal Remedies

1. Colvin, Alexander J.S. "The Growing Use of Mandatory Arbitration." *Economic Policy Institute.* April 6, 2018, https://www.epi.org/publication /the-growing-use-of-mandatory-arbitration-access-to-the-courts-is-now -barred-for-more-than-60-million-american-workers/.
2. Estlund, Cynthia. "The Black Hole of Mandatory Arbitration," *North Carolina Law Review*, vol. 96, 2018, https://scholarship.law.unc.edu/cgi/viewcontent .cgi?article=5972&context=nclr.
3. Colvin, "The Growing Use of Mandatory Arbitration."
4. Harris, Elizabeth A. "Despite #MeToo Glare, Efforts to Ban Secret Settlements Stop Short." *New York Times.* June 15, 2019, https://www.nytimes.com/2019/06 /14/arts/metoo-movement-nda.html.
5. "A Call for Legislative Action to Eliminate Workplace Harassment," October 2018. Issued and signed by thirty-nine organizations, including the ACLU, Leadership Conference on Civil and Human Rights, National Women's Law Center, AFL-CIO, American Association of University Women, NAACP, National Alliance to End Sexual Violence, National Employment Lawyers Association, National Organization for Women Foundation, and YWCA USA.
6. Cornwell, Susan. "Congress Passes Bill to Make Members Pay Sexual Misconduct Claims." Reuters. December 13, 2018, https://www.reuters .com/article/us-usa-congress-harassment/congress-passes-bill-to-make -members-pay-sexual-misconduct-claims-idUSKBN1OC2V0.
7. "Durbin, Duckworth Join Colleagues to Introduce Sweeping Legislation to Address Harassment in the Workplace," press release from the Office of Dick Durbin, April 10, 2019, https://www.durbin.senate.gov/newsroom /press-releases/durbin-duckworth-join-colleagues-to-introduce-sweeping -legislation-to-address-harassment-in-the-workplace.
8. NWLC report: Andrea Johnson, Kathryn Menefee, Ramya Sekaran "Progress in Advancing #MeToo Workplace Reforms in 20 States by 2020." National Women's Law Center. July 2019, https://nwlc.org/resources/ progress-in-advancing-me-too-workplace-reforms-in-20statesby2020/.
9. New international labour standard to combat violence, harassment, at work agreed." International Labour Association news. June 21, 2019, https:// www.ilo.org/ilc/ILCSessions/108/media-centre/news/WCMS_711321 /lang—en/index.htm.

10. "Stop Sexual Harassment in NYC Act: Frequently Asked Questions."

11. Speech at *Atlantic* magazine seminar on workplace inclusion, March 2019.

12. U.S. EEOC, Select Task Force on the Study of Harassment in the Workplace, Report of Co-Chairs Chai R. Feldblum and Victoria A. Lipnic, June 2016, https://www.eeoc.gov/eeoc/task_force/harassment/.

13. Rossein, Merrick. *Employment Discrimination Law and Litigation*, Volume 2, chapter 5, pp. 21–25. Thomson Reuters, 2019 edition.

14. Letter from the New York State Assembly Ethics Committee to Assembly Speaker Carl E. Heastie. November 27, 2017, https://nyassembly.gov/Press/20171129/11–27–17%20letter.pdf.

15. Letter from the New York State Assembly Ethics Committee to Assembly Speaker Carl E. Heastie.

16. Letter from the New York State Assembly Ethics Committee to Assembly Speaker Carl E. Heastie, March 8, 2016, https://nyassembly.gov/Press/20160309a/Ethics%20Committee%203-8-16.pdf.

Chapter 8: Individual Action Steps

1. Stolberg, Sheryl Gay, and Sydney Ember. "Biden's Tactile Politics Threaten His Return in the #MeToo Era." *New York Times*. April 2, 2019, https://www.nytimes.com/2019/04/02/us/politics/joe-biden-women-me-too.html.

2. Carey, Benedict. "Beyond Biden: How Close Is Too Close?" *New York Times*. April 4, 2019, https://www.nytimes.com/2019/04/04/health/psychology-metoo-biden.html.

3. Sellers, Patricia. "The Fall of a Wall Street Highflier." *Fortune*. March 8, 2010, http://archive.fortune.com/2010/03/05/news/companies/erin_callan_lehman_full.fortune/index.htm.

4. La Roche, Julia. "The Spectacular Rise, Fall, and Sudden Return of Erin Callan." Business Insider. March 18, 2013, https://www.businessinsider.com/life-of-erin-callan-2013-3#she-was-considered-a-very-fashionable-and-well-heeled-exec-8.

5. Sellers, Patricia. "Erin Callan, Lehman's Ex-CFO, Goes Public." *Fortune*. February 23, 2011, http://fortune.com/2011/02/22/erin-callan-lehmans-ex-cfo-goes-public/.

6. Hewlett, Sylvia Ann. *Executive Presence*, 79–104.

7. *Sara Tirschwell v. TCW Group Inc. Supreme Court of the State of New York County of New York*. January 25, 2018, https://dlbjbjzgnk95t.cloudfront.net/1005000/1005917/document%20(12).pdf.

8.   Gelles, David. "Wall Street Has Been Unscathed by MeToo. Until Now."
     New York Times. March 16, 2019, https://www.nytimes.com/2019/03/16
     /business/metoo-wall-street-tcw-tirschwell-ravich.html.
9.   Hewlett, Sylvia Ann, et al., *"The Sponsor Effect."*
10. Ember, Sydney, and Jonathan Martin. "Joe Biden, in Video, Says He Will Be
     'More Mindful' of Personal Space." *New York Times*. April 3, 2019, https://
     www.nytimes.com/2019/04/03/us/politics/joe-biden-women-video.html.
11. Ghomeshi, Jian. "Reflections from a Hashtag." *New York Review of Books*.
     October 11, 2018, https://www.nybooks.com/articles/2018/10/11/reflections
     -hashtag/.
12. Ruttenberg, Danya. "Famous Abusers Seek Easy Forgiveness. Rosh
     Hashanah Teaches Us Repentance Is Hard." *Washington Post* blog.
     September 6, 2018, https://www.washingtonpost.com/outlook/famous
     -abusers-seek-easy-forgiveness-rosh-hashanah-teaches-us-repentance
     -is-hard/2018/09/06/c2dc2cac-b0ab-11e8–9a6a-565d92a3585d_story
     .html?utm_term=.e8f9dea9f836.
13. Graf, Nikki. "Sexual Harassment at Work in the Era of #MeToo." Pew
     Research Center's Social & Demographic Trends Project. September 27,
     2018, https://www.pewsocialtrends.org/2018/04/04/sexual-harassment-at
     -work-in-the-era-of-metoo/.
14. Desvaux, Georges, et al. "Women Matter: Ten Years of Insights on Gender
     Diversity." McKinsey & Co. October 2017, https://www.mckinsey.com
     /featured-insights/gender-equality/women-matter-ten-years-of-insights-on
     -gender-diversity.
15. Hewlett, Sylvia Ann, et al. *Innovation, Diversity, and Market Growth*, pp. 2–5.
16. "Stephen R. Howe Jr.—EY." Profiles in Diversity Journal, May 17, 2015,
     http://www.diversityjournal.com/15219-steven-r-howe-jr-ey/.
17. Howe, Steve. "Celebrating Diversity Helps Build a Better Working World
     for All." LinkedIn. Accessed September 16, 2019, https://www.linkedin.
     com/pulse/celebrating-diversity-helps-build-better-working-world-steve-
     howe/.
18. Donnelly, Grace. "Global Diversity Officer at EY Talks Workplace
     Inclusion Post-Election." *Fortune*. November 11, 2016, http://fortune.
     com/2016/11/11/global-diversity-officer-at-ey-talksworkplace-inclusion-
     post-election/.
19. Sullivan, Jay. "Think 'Engagement': Advice From The C-Suite." *Forbes*.
     February 9, 2017, https://www.forbes.com/sites/jaysullivan/2017/02/09/
     think-engagement-advice-from-the-c-suite/#193890c1abe0.

Chapter 9: Company Action Steps

1. Coffee, Patrick. "IPG CEO Issues Memo Promising 'Zero Tolerance' for Sexual Harassment." *Adweek.* October 30, 2017, https://www.adweek.com /agencies/ipg-ceo-issues-memo-promising-zero-tolerance-for-sexual -harassment/.
2. Peifer, Karri, and John Ramsey. "Amid New Allegations of Misconduct, 17 Former Employees Discuss the Culture at the Martin Agency." *Richmond-Times Dispatch.* December 15, 2017, https://www.richmond.com/business /local/amid-new-allegations-of-misconduct-former-employees-discuss-the -culture/article_b0930ee2-c672–55d6–8aca-ef14836999d9.html.
3. Coffee, Patrick. "IPG CEO Michael Roth Cites 'Swift Disciplinary Action' on #MeToo in New Letter to Shareholders." *Adweek.* April 12, 2018, https://www.adweek.com/agencyspy/ipg-ceo-michael-roth-cites-swift -disciplinary-action-on-metoo-in-new-letter-to-shareholders/145809.
4. Galunic, Charles. "Does Articulating Your Corporate Values Matter?" INSEAD Knowledge. July 1, 2015, https://knowledge.insead.edu/leadership -organisations/does-articulating-your-corporate-values-matter-4126.
5. Khosrowshahi, Dara. "Uber's New Cultural Norms." LinkedIn. November 7, 2017, https://www.linkedin.com/pulse/ubers-new-cultural-norms -dara-khosrowshahi/?trk=aff_src.aff-lilpar_c.partners_pkw.10078_net .mediapartner_plc.Skimbit%20Ltd._pcrid.449670_learning&veh=aff_src .aff-lilpar_c.partners_pkw.10078_net.mediapartner_plc.Skimbit%20Ltd ._pcrid.449670_learning&irgwc=1.
6. Tippett, Elizabeth C. "CBS' Moonves Scandal Shows Why Corporate America Needs Tougher CEO Pay Contracts." *The Conversation.* December 19, 2018, https://theconversation.com/cbs-moonves-scandal-shows-why -corporate-america-needs-tough"er-ceo-pay-contracts-109050.
7. McGregor, Jena. "After Sexual Harassment Cases, Fidelity's CEO Has Moved Her Office Close to Fund Managers." *Washington Post.* November 22, 2017, https://www.washingtonpost.com/news/on-leadership/wp/2017 /11/22/after-sexual-harassment-cases-fidelitys-ceo-has-moved-her-office -close-to-fund-managers/?utm_term=.9224b82e7854.
8. Stahl, Leslie. "Leading by Example to Close the Gender Pay Gap." CBS News. April 15, 2018, https://www.cbsnews.com/news/salesforce-ceo-marc-benioff -leading-by-example-to-close-the-gender-pay-gap/.
9. Smith, David G., and W. Brad Johnson. "Lots of Men Are Gender-Equality Allies in Private. Why Not in Public?" *Harvard Business Review.* October

13, 2017, https://hbr.org/2017/10/lots-of-men-are-gender-equality-allies
-in-private-why-not-in-public.

10. Jane Mayer. "The Case of Al Franken." *New Yorker.* July 29, 2019, https://
www.newyorker.com/magazine/2019/07/29/the-case-of-al-franken.

11. Ayres, Ian. "Information Escrows." *Yale Law School Legal Scholarship
Repository.* 2012, http://digitalcommons.law.yale.edu/fss_papers/4741.

12. "A Reckoning in Our Own House." WNYC. December 5, 2017, https://
www.wnycstudios.org/story/otm-reckoning-our-own-house.

13. "Deloitte Helps Show the Way on Harassment." Editorial Board. *Financial
Times.* December 16, 2018, https://www.ft.com/content/95252f5c-ffa2
-11e8-ac00-57a2a826423e.

14. Goodstein, Laurie, and Sharon Otterman. "Catholic Priests Abused 1,000
Children in Pennsylvania, Report Says." *New York Times.* August 14, 2018,
https://www.nytimes.com/2018/08/14/us/catholic-church-sex-abuse
-pennsylvania.html.

15. Povoledo, Elisabetta, and Sharon Otterman. "Cardinal Theodore McCarrick
Resigns Amid Sexual Abuse Scandal." *New York Times.* July 28, 2018,
https://www.nytimes.com/2018/07/28/world/europe/cardinal-theodore
-mccarrick-resigns.html; Burke, Daniel. "US Catholic Bishops Announce
New Policies to Police Bishops." CNN. September 19, 2018, https://www
.cnn.com/2018/09/19/us/catholic-bishops-new-abuse-policy/index.html.

16. "Is There a Better Way to Handle Workplace Sexual Harassment?"
Knowledge at Wharton. University of Pennsylvania. April 12, 2018, http://
knowledge.wharton.upenn.edu/article/better-way-handle-workplace-sexual
-harassment/.

17. Moffett, Andrea Turner. *Harness the Power of the Purse* (Los Angeles, Rare
Bird Books, 2015).

18. Hewlett, Sylvia Ann, et al. "Innovation, Diversity, and Market Growth." p. 4.

19. Hewlett, Sylvia Ann, et al. "Innovation, Diversity, and Market Growth."
p. 5.

20. "'You Have to Have a Plan to Deal with Them': How the Media Fell Out
of Love with Beto O'Rourke." *Vanity Fair.* May 15, 2019, https://www.
vanityfair.com/news/2019/05/how-the-media-fell-out-of-love-with-beto-
orourke.

21. "Chart of Risk Factors for Harassment and Responsive Strategies," U.S.
Equal Employment Opportunity Commission, https://www.eeoc.gov/eeoc/
task_force/harassment/risk-factors.cfm.

INDEX